Beyond
Left and Right

A publication of
the Center for Self-Governance

Beyond
Left and Right

Breaking the Political Stalemate

A. Lawrence Chickering

ICS PRESS
Institute for Contemporary Studies
San Francisco, California

This book is a publication of the Center for Self-Governance, which is dedicated to the study of self-governing institutions. The Center is affiliated with the Institute for Contemporary Studies, a nonpartisan, nonprofit, public policy research organization. The analyses, conclusions, and opinions expressed in ICS Press publications are those of the authors and not necessarily those of the Institute for Contemporary Studies, the Institute's officers or directors, or others associated with or funding its work.

Inquiries should be addressed to ICS Press, Institute for Contemporary Studies, 243 Kearny Street, San Francisco, CA 94108. (415) 981-5353. Fax (415) 986-4878. For book orders and catalog requests call toll-free within the United States: (800) 326-0263. Distributed to the trade by National Book Network, Lanham, Maryland.

Library of Congress Cataloging-in-Publication Data
Chickering, A. Lawrence.
    Beyond left and right : breaking the political stalemate / A. Lawrence Chickering.
        p.   cm.
    Includes bibliographical references and index.
    ISBN 1-55815-209-1
    1. Decentralization in government—United States. 2. Neighborhood government—United States. 3. Community power—United States. 4. Political participation—United States. 5. Right and left (Political science)   I. Title.
JS341.C48 1993
320.973—dc20   92-47007
                                                                          CIP

To Serena

Contents

Foreword

Politics in America is not working. Trivial disputes flare and subside without reaching resolution. Fundamental problems linger, unaddressed. We, the American people, are desperate for "change." We see the government at all levels as *the* problem solver—yet at the same time we doubt its ability to do anything well. All too often, we find ourselves forestalled from improving our own communities by the regulations of an intrusive or inert state. We have reached a political stalemate.

The reason for all this is that we have neglected the fundamental, even constitutional, crisis in our politics. The concentration of power in the hands of government bureaucrats has made "dependents" out of free citizens. The bureaucratic welfare state has taken away the sense that we are responsible as citizens to share in our own governance—the state of mind that once made America a *participatory* democracy. Without the unity of purpose that comes from working together to govern ourselves, we have too often lapsed into apathy or gravitated toward strident factions of "left" and "right," each insisting that a distant government satisfy its parochial demands.

Lawry Chickering confronts this situation head on. Noting that our political crisis results, in large measure, from the disempowerment of citizens, Chickering urges a change of national course. America's disparate people can share in a revived, all-inclusive political community, he writes, only if we build that community *ourselves,* through self-governance and entrepreneurship.

Beyond Left and Right is more than a fulmination against political paralysis. It is also a work of hope, laying an intellectual foundation for the reconstruction, by countless self-reliant and enterprising citizens and their communities, of American democracy as it was originally envisaged. If we grasp the power to resolve the problems that beset our own communities, we can restore a fully functioning politics—and at the same time overcome the social bitterness that now divides and frustrates us.

Lawry Chickering and I have been partners for a number of years at the Institute for Contemporary Studies and its affiliate, the International Center for Economic Growth, working to promote the self-governing and entrepreneurial ideal in America and around the world. We share a desire to help people realize that they possess the capacity, the right, and the duty to take responsibility for their own lives. *Beyond Left and Right* is a vitally important statement of this vision, a guide to rethinking the issues—our shared problems and their possible solutions—as our society moves forward.

Robert B. Hawkins, Jr., Ph.D.
President
Institute for Contemporary Studies

Acknowledgments

The ideas in this book are the product of many years' contemplation of problems and puzzles that lurk beneath the surface of our political debate but never seem to break it. The book has gone through many revisions, some of them so great that the people who read and commented on earlier drafts may not recognize what remained when I had finished responding to their criticisms. In the final stages, encouraged by my editors, I even dropped substantial portions of earlier drafts, and am holding them for inclusion in a second book on the issues introduced in the postscript. For all of these reasons, the convention of excusing other people from responsibility for the author's ideas applies with particular force here.

A number of people read and commented on part or all of earlier drafts, and I want to thank them. They include John Baden, Eugene Bardach, Adam Bellow, Michael Boskin, John E. Coons, Robert Davis, Gus di Zerega, Milton Friedman, the late William Havender, Seymour Martin Lipset, Stephen Schwartz, Paul Weaver, Richard White, and Aaron Wildavsky. I want to thank Joan Chatfield Taylor for helping me with the research on cultural changes during the 1960s. And I want to extend special thanks for special encouragements I received over a number of years from Thomas Lipscomb and from my agent, Gerald Lubenow.

I also want to acknowledge conversations—some of them going back a number of years—with countless people whose influence was important in a multitude of ways. They include Michael Brown, William F. Buckley, Jr., my brother Nick Chickering, Hernando de Soto, Herbert Gold, Gertrude Himmelfarb, Muzammel Huq, Julian Jaynes, Irving Kristol, Leon Louw, Henry Lucas, Jr., John Marks, Adam Meyerson, Michael Murphy, Robert Nisbet, Stephen

Rhinesmith, Richard Rodriguez, Jurgen Ruesch, the late Mohamed Salahdine, Jack Sarfatti, the late Paul Seabury, Larry Silberman, Ricky Silberman, Thomas Sowell, and David Wise.

I want to express thanks to Michael Joyce and the John M. Olin Foundation for their early support, which made the book possible; and also to the Earhart Foundation for additional assistance that allowed me to complete the project.

I want to give special recognition to the extraordinary contacts I had with the late Franz Winkler, whose influenced me in crucial ways on certain basic issues. I want to thank Michael Briand for an extraordinary conceptual edit he did on an earlier draft. I am also grateful to my secretary, Colleen Doane, who provided important assistance in final preparation of the manuscript.

I want to thank my colleague Robert B. Hawkins, Jr., president of ICS, for his help and encouragement in innumerable ways over many years; and I want also to recognize the herculean editing job done by Peter Hayes. I shudder to think of the life expectancy he invested in the process.

Finally above all, I want to thank my wife and best friend, Serena, for her help, encouragement, and unutterable patience as this book, which must have seemed like a shaggy dog story, followed its course.

Beyond
Left and Right

Prologue

T oward the end of his book *Good-Bye, Darkness,* William Manchester relates the nightmare of the U.S. Marines' fight for Okinawa, the last battle of World War II before the planned invasion of Japan. His friends are dying all around him—there is blood and carnage everywhere. He looks at the hideous reality, and something inside him snaps: the bond between him and the Marine Corps. Disillusion sets in. He writes of his contempt for the "tacky appeals to patriotism" in "The Marines' Hymn," as he sees through the "Corps' swagger" and the "ruthless exploitation" of the loyalty pledged in boot camp. He will fight on and continue to do the job, but his passion and idealism are gone.

Moments later, he is wounded—superficially, but enough to remove him from the field and send him to hospital. It is a "million-dollar wound, the dream of every infantryman." But later, as he lies in the safety of his hospital bed, eating hot food on clean plates and listening to rebroadcasts of radio programs from the States, he learns that his unit has been ordered to attempt an amphibious assault behind Japanese lines. So he jumps hospital, goes AWOL, and rejoins his unit.

He could not account for his behavior—until thirty-five years later, when he returned to Okinawa to research the book. "It was an act of love," he writes. "Those men on the line were my family, my home. They were closer to me than I can say, closer than any friends had been or ever would be. They had never let me down, and I couldn't do it to them."

These words are almost incomprehensible today, especially for the generation of Americans who did not know World War II, for those whose only real war was Vietnam. For my parents' generation too, the generation that lived through the Great Depression and "The War" as they called it, these words seem strange because the world they describe is now a distant memory. People who remember World War II cannot fathom how what they knew so well and took for granted was lost, how things could have changed so much in so short a time.

Manchester's world was devoted to the traditional virtues: duty, honor, sacrifice. In that world good and evil were clear, patriotism was nothing to be ashamed of, roles were well defined. The traditional authority of family and church was strong, and the word "responsibility" defined and symbolized a way of life for most people.

I was born in early 1941, about ten months before Pearl Harbor. I recall Manchester's world vaguely, and I have a distinct sense of how it began to collapse. Growing up, memories of the war were still strong (we were reminded constantly of children starving in Europe), and much of that world was still intact. Through the 1950s, even as late as 1962, when I graduated from college, traditional values and roles still governed most of what we did. In 1962, most people still got married in their early twenties and stayed that way for a lifetime. They focused their lives—as people used to say—on getting a "good job" in order to "make good."

That world started to unravel around 1960, and it has continued to do so for three decades.

This unraveling has had a number of important consequences. One of the most striking is that it has undermined and greatly damaged the coherence of American political life, destroying in the process much of the confidence that people feel in our politics. The result is a crisis in our political culture that is occurring, ironically, just at the moment when the American system of democratic capitalism has completed a triumphant ideological victory over its principal adversary, Marxism-Leninism.

The admission of communism's failures by the new leaders of

Russia and other former Soviet republics has ended the ideological competition that had ravaged geopolitics since the end of World War II. Despite this great victory, many people in the United States believe that they have little to show for their triumph. They can find no spoils to enjoy. People across the political spectrum agree that at its moment of triumph, American liberal democracy suffers problems of its own so serious that no one feels like celebrating.

Although conservatives and liberals point to very different examples of America's troubles, the sense is felt across the political spectrum that something is deeply wrong. For liberals the sickness is revealed in the growing problems of the homeless and the underclass, in Wall Street cheating, and the violation of trust between the executive and legislative branches over Irangate. Conservatives see decay in rising rates of crime and illegitimacy, and in declining standards of educational achievement.

Other indicators of social disintegration lend themselves less to use in the ideological debate—the divorce rate, which continues to rise; the decline of political party affiliation; the deep disaffection from the mainline churches; the spread of drug and alcohol abuse and related emotional disorders such as depression; and a whole variety of phenomena implying adolescent alienation, including the enormous recent increase in urban gang violence and rising rates of teen suicide, homicide, illegitimacy, and delinquency. Even surveys of people's perceptions of personal happiness and honesty in our society show marked declines over the last several decades.

It is not surprising that these signs of social distress are greatly affecting our politics. Under these circumstances, a 1992 Democratic presidential ticket featuring two relative kids—likeable young candidates who are plainly not part of the old politics—had an enormous advantage over an incumbent president whose desperation to rediscover a "vision" for the future pushed him to turn over his party's convention to the control of the religious right.

The signs of trouble in our politics have not been lost on the general public. In the mid-1960s public confidence in American institutions began a long-term decline that affected government, business, labor, education, and medicine. Although this decline was slowed during the Reagan presidency, Irangate dashed hopes that confidence might revive. Victory in the Gulf War enormously improved President George Bush's approval ratings in early 1991, but by that year's end his popularity had plummeted.

While conservatives and liberals view our troubles differently, both sides see a fundamental crisis of values—a personal and social crisis of understanding how we can affirm our highest purposes, and even whether we have any such purposes.

Our crisis of values is caused by our deep-seated, philosophical uncertainty about what values are true—by our uncertainty about whether any values can be known to be true. The late Allan Bloom wrote about this problem, in the first pages of *The Closing of the American Mind,* in terms of the moral relativism that is rampant on university campuses. The problem was emphasized to me at the centennial anniversary of a private secondary school that had been an all-boys' institution when I attended it in the 1950s. Sitting on a panel that was deliberating how to teach values to adolescents, I was struck by the ambivalence that several members expressed as to whether the moral tone of our society had improved or regressed since the school's founding. They lamented the decline of traditional values such as civility, trust, and humility (although no one actually used the latter word, it serves better than any other to represent the bundle of qualities we have lost). But it was clear their complaint was more complicated when two of them noted the absence of any women or minority-group members on our panel, which suggested they thought the school was still dominated by a retrograde past, contaminated by sexism and racism.

It struck me as odd that none of the alumni protested this implicit criticism of the school's moral past. It was hard to avoid the conclusion that no one there—although they represented the entire political spectrum—had any firm idea whether our culture has moved forward or backward morally. One could only conclude that they felt the decline of traditional values was both to be lamented and celebrated.

There was a reason for the lack of serious discussion of the issue that day. To paraphrase the conclusion of Alasdair MacIntyre, in his 1981 book *After Virtue:* our moral consensus has collapsed, and we lack the terms of argument to persuade each other about the great political and moral issues we face. So we say nothing.

We have lost many of our common touchstones for determining truth, and, as MacIntyre notes, protest has therefore become the principal form of expression in our political life.

Having lost our consensus about what is true, we have no way to speak or appeal to our responsibilities or obligations to each other. Instead, our political vocabulary concerns itself with rights, sneaking appeals to social responsibility through a polemical back door. Our courts are thus jammed with people claiming their rights and other people's responsibilities. In the debate over abortion, for example, both sides rest their claims on individual rights—the woman's right to choose against the fetus or unborn child's right to live. No one appeals to the individual's moral obligation because no one knows how. The terms do not exist anymore for such discourse.

Our obsession with rights occurs because we have lost our ability to talk about obligations. Until we rediscover how to appeal to obligations—to the values that connect us—our frivolous appeal to rights cannot decline and may even increase.

Without society's agreement on what is true, the decline of society is unavoidable. And without our knowing what is true, we are in deep conflict over what to do about our plight. This is the dilemma we face when we wonder "why things aren't the way they used to be."

The loss of consensus about basic values has scarred our political and social life since the end of the 1960s. For more than twenty years I have watched the controversy from one side. I first became professionally involved in this debate in 1968, working as assistant to the editor of *National Review,* the magazine founded and edited by William F. Buckley, Jr. In 1970, my vantage point as a conservative shifted to Sacramento and the California State Office of Economic Opportunity, under Governor Ronald Reagan. And since 1974 I have been associated with the Institute for Contemporary Studies, a San Francisco-based "neoconservative" think tank that I helped found with a number of people close to Governor Reagan.

My public policy career began at a time (1968) when authority was everywhere under attack, when the country was coming apart in every way—socially, politically, culturally. It was several weeks after the Tet Offensive in Vietnam, hours before the assassination of Dr. Martin Luther King, Jr. It was the heyday of acid rock and the Fillmore Auditorium, Haight Ashbury, and the Chicago Seven—a time when the country was swept by radical political forces and was tormented by political conflict. It is difficult to relate what that period was like to anyone who missed it. How can one recapture the experience of leaning out a window at the Conrad Hilton Hotel in Chicago at three o'clock in the morning in August 1968 during the Democratic convention and listening to the angry chanting: "Hey, hey, LBJ! How many kids did you kill today?" There has been nothing remotely like it since, and I feel its passing—as do many people of my generation across the political spectrum—with an odd combination of disappointment and relief.

The race riots of the late 1960s finally subsided; the Vietnam War wound down. The country seemed calmer again. In 1971, it was clear things were changing when a sentimental film, *Love Story,* became the most popular of the year.

The conflict seemed gradually to subside through the 1970s and into the 1980s. But when open political warfare broke out over Irangate and the Supreme Court confirmation hearings of Judge Robert Bork at the end of the Reagan years, it became clear that the calm had been only a mirage.

Throughout these two decades, I have watched this conflict and have wondered why there was no real dialogue between opponents. Opponents used to be able to talk to each other without exchanging accusations of terminal immorality, or so I remember. Even on issues that seem to defy solution—issues such as homelessness, drug addiction, the persistent poverty of the underclass, and the decline of the sense of personal responsibility and obligation to others—people on all sides of every issue talk as if they know everything, when it is obvious they (and we) know very little.

Opponents today rarely acknowledge commonalities of interest. They rarely acknowledge weaknesses in their own arguments. In a recent symposium in the *National Interest* on the subject of *glasnost,* several participants predicted that the loss of Marxism as a foil will force advocates of democracy to express their beliefs in positive terms. But this will not be easy. Our preoccupation with exposing falsehood as the means of defining truth has relieved us from the burden of having to examine ourselves and affirm our beliefs in a positive way. Even critics of *The Closing of the American Mind,* who could have conducted a serious, elevated debate on the crisis of values, dodged this issue and attacked author Bloom for his "elitism." In doing so, they focused on disagreements that were trivial compared to much larger areas of agreement between left and right over the decline of values.

The lack of real dialogue is intensified because the principal words and concepts we use do not mean anything concrete. Even words like "conservative" and "liberal" have come to mean so many conflicting things that coherent talk about politics has become all but impossible. Without a vocabulary that speaks clearly, it is impossible to have a serious discussion, even about trivial things. Without such a vocabulary, it is impossible even to know whether we are as divided as we appear to be.

How can the word "conservative" mean anything coherent when it supposedly describes both Milton Friedman and the Moral Majority? How can one make sense of a word that describes Friedman's libertarian commitment to the modernist values of individualism, freedom, reason, and progress, and the Moral Majority's diagnosis of the modern torment as being caused by the assault of those same (liberal/libertarian) values on traditional virtues? How could one exaggerate the differences between these ideas, all of which are said to be conservative?

"Liberal" is no more meaningful; it can signify almost anything today. It includes both the commitment of the American Civil Liberties Union (ACLU) to individualism, freedom, and rights, and the environmentalists' critique of excessive individualism and embrace of obligations beyond the self. Among liberals can be found both those who favor reason and those who oppose reason; both those who favor progress and resist it. Liberals may want centralization of political functions, and they may also want decentralization. Liberals include both anarchists and members of the counterculture. Some are fiercely individualistic and opposed to all government interference in individual life, and some are socialists, whose passion, appealing to "justice," is to use the government to force people to be good.

It serves no purpose to examine political behavior in hopes of finding coherence. What would be proved if it turned out that Friedman and members of the Moral Majority voted for the same presidential candidates? The question is *why* do such odd bedfellows, embracing such different ideas, vote for the same candidates, read the same magazines, like the same newspaper columnists, and read the same political books?

The longer one ponders the words "conservative" and "liberal," the more one suspects that each means nothing more than "not-the-other." If all "conservative" means is "not liberal," and vice versa, then it becomes easy to see why serious political debate is impossible.

With the central words in our political vocabulary meaning so much and so little, it is no wonder that so many people, both conservatives and liberals, begin claiming betrayal the day after one of their own has been elected to office. Considering how many conflicting things these labels mean, it could not be otherwise.

In this book I will argue that the failure to mount a serious discussion of our crisis of values has less to do with actual differences between political groupings than with how we approach major issues. Whatever may have been true in the past, our political vocabulary no longer speaks to the major issues we face. The problem of the vocabulary we use is related to the reasons we are struggling.

All of this presents an intellectual challenge that must be solved if any of the major ideological positions are to regain coherence and value. The challenge is how to reconcile and integrate our traditional commitments to individual freedom and rights with a sense of values beyond the self and a commitment to the larger good. This dilemma is distinctive to the American experience, but it is spreading everywhere in the world.

The nature of the dilemma explains a lot about the incoherence of our political debate, as each ideological grouping struggles to integrate a freedom side and an order side—the one side focusing only on the rights of the individual and the other focusing only on obligations to the community. Almost no one, in fact, solely embraces either freedom or order, unleavened by the other. But, unsure how to acknowledge the "opposite" value without giving up some of their own value's cogency, all ideological factions cling to the extreme positions that now dominate our political life.

The dilemma caused by uncertainty about how to integrate freedom and order is as preoccupying to conservatives as it is to liberals. On one side, the impulse to freedom provided the spark that ignited *glasnost* and *perestroika* in the Soviet Union; it underlay the Chinese students' protests for democracy in Tiananmen Square; and it is changing traditional societies everywhere. At the same time, throughout Western political systems, there is concern that the values of order, virtue, community, and belonging are in crisis.

No matter how we emphasize the differences between most political opponents, the commonality of their quest to integrate freedom and order is far more important. As modern people, whether on the left or the right, we cannot live without freedom *and* order. Reconciling these ideals is crucial to solving the crisis of values that will otherwise overwhelm our civilization and all we hold dear.

1

Freedom and Order

In his visit to the United States in 1831, Alexis de Tocqueville observed an extraordinary marriage of individualism and voluntary association that marked the American character. This combination of what I call freedom and order was almost unknown in Europe at that time, but it goes back to the founding of the United States as what Seymour Martin Lipset has called the "first new nation." Today, however, our commitment to order (voluntary association) is breaking down, and we face the need to rediscover our sense of responsibility.

This challenge confronts both society as a whole and individuals, forcing them to puzzle and agonize about what to do with the precious freedom that they and their ancestors fought so hard for. People in the United States demand freedom—the right to control their own lives and destinies, independent of either political or moral authority; but they also continue to need order—connections to other people, larger ideals, things beyond themselves. At the heart of the freedom/order problem, then, is the quest to develop institutions that will encourage individuals and groups to be "self-governing."

Self-governance is a principle that implies empowerment of both

9

individuals and political and social groups to control their own affairs, independent of commands from higher authorities. A self-governing system includes various complex arrangements whereby individual citizens can voluntarily cooperate to achieve common purposes. These arrangements may cover many different activities, from market exchanges of private goods to voluntary participation in managing common-pool resources, such as water, land, fisheries, and so on. Two concepts are important in any self-governing system: *entrepreneurship,* implying individual freedom, initiative, and creativity; and *cooperation,* emphasizing working together for the common good. Both freedom *and* order.

The dilemma of self-governance is most evident in advanced, industrialized democracies such as the United States, where individualism has developed furthest, and where tradition has most lost its grip. Adolescence is the proper metaphor for the current condition of these societies: having let go of tradition (their "parental" authority), they now look for ways to live as "adults."

If the search to integrate freedom and order is the dominant impulse within the major political groupings in the American political system, the solution to all major policy issues also now depends on it. Whether the issue is poverty, race, the environment, women's rights—you name it—the solution depends on finding a response to the larger challenge of integrating freedom and order.

The American Historical Experience

Alexander Hamilton made clear the nature of the challenge faced by the American Founding Fathers when he emphasized it in the opening paragraph of essay 1 of *The Federalist.* "[T]he people of this country," he wrote,

> must decide the important question, whether societies of men are really capable or not of establishing good government from reflection and choice, or whether they are forever destined to depend for their political constitutions on accident and force.

A few lines later he focused on the crux of the issue: "Happy will it be if our choice should be directed by a judicious estimate of our true interests, unperplexed and unbiased by considerations not connected with the public good." The challenge for societies is freely to choose the obligations ("our true interests") that are necessary for good government. The challenge is the same for individuals.

Half a century later, Tocqueville saw a partial solution to Hamilton's quandary in the voluntary association he found everywhere in this country. But he remained deeply concerned. "The prestige of royal power has vanished," he wrote in his classic *Democracy in America,* "but has not been replaced by the majesty of the law; nowadays the people dispute authority but fear it, and more is dragged from them by fear than was formerly granted through respect and love." Therefore, he called for a "new political science" to establish new sources of authority and values, and encourage individual responsibility.

Tocqueville's distress at what he saw in America 150 years ago precisely anticipated our current dilemma. He expressed his concern in terms that anticipated the despair many on both the left and right feel over the present-day crisis of values:

> Have all ages been like ours? And have men always dwelt in a world in which nothing is connected? Where virtue is without genius, and genius without honor? Where love of order is confused with a tyrant's tastes, and the sacred cult of freedom is taken as scorn of law? Where conscience sheds but doubtful light on human actions? Where nothing any longer seems either forbidden or permitted, honest or dishonorable, true or false?[1]

Our commitment to integrate individualism and free choice with a moral and social vision of the good life is central to our politics, as Tocqueville suggested, because each value is incomplete without the others. They are complementary values, because freedom without obligation or virtue is nihilism, and obligation or virtue without freedom is authoritarianism.* An integration of these values leads to the ultimate ideal of conservatives and liberals alike: that individuals, left free, will choose the good.

---

*It has often been said that the United States is committed to freedom and equality. For the latter principle I prefer to substitute words like "obligation" and "order," which I take to refer to something much larger—a whole collection of values, only one of which is equality in its purest sense. Other related values include community, virtue, brotherhood; these words together evoke the spirit with which people treat each other.

Adolescence as Metaphor

Anyone who has been a parent knows the preoccupying human question, which appears early in every child's life: Why? Parents also know just how difficult, finally, it is to answer.

This question does not leave us after adolescence, and its persistence explains why demands for freedom have grown and traditional obligations (those based on unquestioning faith) have declined. It also explains why we must find new sources of authority and values that satisfy our need to understand.

Philosophy and religion share an important agreement about the underlying problem. Philosophy describes it in terms of the desire, intrinsic to human nature, for freedom and knowledge—freedom from tradition and habit, knowledge validated by experience. In philosophy these desires can be fulfilled by searching for truth through reason. Socrates provided the model of this quest, and he died for his commitment, which the authorities of Athens regarded as subversive and dangerous.

Similarly, the yearning for knowledge and the related need for freedom are also among the basic themes of the creation myths of all the world's great religions. The central purpose of all but the most primitive religions is to account for man's departure from the divine plan and the terms of his return to it.

Although religion and philosophy both see the search for knowledge as the central problem, they seem to propose different solutions: faith and reason, respectively. Some philosophers, however, have argued that philosophy and religion are more alike than we are used to believing, both in how they pose this issue and how they formulate the answer to it.[2]

For the purposes of this book, we may employ adolescence as a metaphor for the stage in the life of a person or a society when the demand for freedom and knowledge begins to overwhelm traditions that were previously accepted on faith. As in the adolescence of an individual, the desire for knowledge implies the demand for freedom. In passing from childhood to adulthood, adolescents rebel against their parents—reject tradition—in a search for knowledge, for values they can call their own. In their journey of self-discovery, their rejection of tradition is not substantive; it is instrumental. People do, after all, for the most part, return to their parents' values. But the transition to conscious awareness of moral and spiritual life defines the very nature of passing to adulthood. The need to search for knowledge is inspired by an increasing consciousness of self, which brings with it a corresponding burden to live by conscious choice, free from preconscious habit. Seeking knowledge, therefore, means not only deciding which values to live by; it also means living a conscious life.

A search for knowledge, like the adolescent's journey, implies that freedom and order must conflict: the search for a new form of order (which will define adult life) implies *negative* freedom from the old order (parental values). Once knowledge is attained, however, the result is a *positive* kind of psychological freedom. It is the freedom experienced by all people who have strong purpose and meaning in their lives—by those whose lives show a strong sense of both personal and social responsibility.

These principles operate individually, socially, and politically, and the challenges associated with them affect us in both individual and group life.

A Modern, Western Problem

Despite antecedents since prehistory, the search for knowledge and the attendant conflict between freedom and obligation is a peculiarly modern problem. "Before the Reformation," wrote Lord Hugh Cecil, "it is impossible to distinguish conservatism in politics, not because there was none, but because there was nothing else."[3]

For the same reason, the conflict between freedom and obligation is not yet a great problem in Asian or African societies, where individualism is still weak, and where obligation to the community still takes precedence over freedom. But the students' rebellion in Tiananmen Square shows how quickly things are changing, even in traditional societies.

In his classic history, *Civilization of the Renaissance in Italy,* the nineteenth-century historian Jacob Burckhardt dates the beginnings of the change I describe from the thirteenth century, when modern individualism made its first appearance on the historical stage.

The conflict between freedom and order has since grown enormously, especially during and after the 1960s. My mother likes to say that the trouble with "my" generation—meaning the generation that grew up after World War II and had no direct experience of the

world of William Manchester's youth—is that we "think too much."
We don't accept things, don't let them alone. Our confusion, of
course, is the price of the freedom we demand. For many, it is a very
high price—some would say prohibitively high—symbolized by
the decline of all forms of tradition during the 1960s.

The efforts of an adolescent to become an adult illuminate our
struggles with freedom today. The freedom that comes with moving
away from parents is frightening, and it often brings with it new
forms of community and order: the teenage gang is only one, extreme form of grouping that shelters adolescents in their exposed
and lonely new condition. Modern societies exhibit a similar search
for new forms of order, especially in political movements such as
environmentalism, the women's movement, and contemporary concern about health and safety.

It may be helpful to consider the dilemma of integrating freedom
and order in terms of additional sets of polarities, whose relationship
may address the same fundamental issues. While these polarities
may appear at first to represent unrelated parts of human experience, the more one considers them and their relation to each other,
the easier it is to see them as posing the same basic challenge.

Order	Freedom
Community	Individualism
Society	Self
Objectivity	Subjectivity
Obligations	Rights
Authority	Liberty
Hierarchy	Equality
Conservatism	Liberalism
Aristocracy	Democracy
Socialism	Capitalism
Faith	Reason
Religion	Science

The list could go on to include polarities drawn from additional
spheres of knowledge.

While many things distinguish the values in the two columns
from each other, each has an outstanding distinguishing characteristic in relation to the value directly opposite it: the ideas in the first

column all characterize the preindividuated, "connected" state of traditional society; the ideas in the second column are all associated with the separate, individuated personality found in more modern societies. Therefore, although it is difficult to relate some of the values within a single column (for example, reason and subjectivity), they characterize a common state of mind, compared with their opposites (faith and objectivity). Capitalism thrives on individualism, especially individual entrepreneurship; socialism represents an attempt to restore community and authority. This explains why socialism appears in the same column as conservatism.

It is important to note that if the ideas in the freedom column are considered only negatively—if individualism is seen as freedom from community, the self as freedom from society—no integration of the columns is possible. Integrating them requires finding a positive understanding of the concepts in the freedom column. Another way of putting this is to say that the ideas in the freedom column can most usefully be understood as conscious means to achieve the values opposite them. Thus a positive understanding of freedom (and its set of values) would be one that leads people freely to choose order (and its set of values). That is the challenge of integrating freedom and order: to find a vision of order that will attract free and conscious commitment.

The dilemma of freedom may be considered as concerning every item in the second column. We are driven to want freedom (individualism, rights, etc.)—we demand it—and this explains our crisis of values; yet we also need order (community, a sense of purpose and belonging) for freedom to be tolerable. Dostoyevsky's meditation on the psychological problem of freedom in the legend of the Grand Inquisitor in *The Brothers Karamazov* explains why so many intellectuals in modern times have embraced authoritarian and even totalitarian politics: because more than any other group (except possibly artists) intellectuals tend to be alienated from tradition, especially religious tradition; and many of them have looked (desperately) to politics for the purpose and meaning they can no longer find in tradition.

The dilemma of freedom and order operates both individually and politically, pushing people to want self-governance both in their personal lives and in their institutions. Yet in practice the distinction between the personal and the political begins to disappear, as the self-governance of individuals is reflected in their work in community with others.

Freedom, Order, and Contemporary Politics

Defining the political left and right became a problem in the late nineteenth century when liberalism began to take on a new and contradictory meaning. The original liberalism, dating from the early nineteenth century, referred to the Lockean belief in protecting individual liberty against the state. It was thus associated with laissez-faire economics. Later, however, English liberal theorists such as Matthew Arnold and T. H. Green developed a broader theory of liberty, encouraging state intervention to relieve poverty and promote social welfare. In the United States, which had never had a conservative tradition in the European sense, "conservative" came to connote a combination of the original tradition of European liberalism and a commitment to traditional moral and social authority—family, church, and local community. "Liberal," in America, came to stand for the later European *étatiste* tradition, and for a commitment to freedom from the traditional social and moral order.

As a result, the American concepts of conservativism and liberalism each acquired qualities of freedom and order, leaving contemporary politics with *four* rather than two contending political ideas. The left and right each divided into two sets of ideas—one embracing freedom, individualism, and rights; and the other supporting virtue, order, community, and equality. Conservatism is therefore divided into libertarian (freedom conservative) and traditionalist (order conservative) parts; and liberalism includes freedom liberals (anarchists, the counterculture, civil libertarians) and order liberals (socialists, welfare state liberals).

The conflict between these two sets of ideas within the left and right—one set (order, community, virtue) coming to us from the ancients, the other (freedom, individualism, rights) appearing only in modern times—has come to infect all of the major terms in our political vocabulary. This conflict is also evident in disputed definitions of "capitalism," "socialism," and other basic staples of our political discourse.

The need to reconcile and integrate these ideas is not only important theoretically; it is also crucial to accomplishing the most practical challenges of governing. For liberals, the key question of governance may be: How can the order (or social democratic) left hope to use the government's powers to achieve social justice when the freedom left (for example, the ACLU), in its commitment to freedom and individual rights, unrelentingly undermines citizens' trust and confidence in government? And in their turn, how can Republicans and conservatives expand personal freedom—which they argue is under threat from welfare state liberalism—when the order right pushes for using government coercion to enforce traditional standards of personal morality?

The dilemma of freedom and order appeared in the American experience because of our historical commitment to freedom from the old European order. Two centuries of increasing individual freedom have delivered us to the crisis of values (that is, of order) that we now face. Our challenge is now to rediscover an order to which we can freely commit ourselves—a self-governing order.

As we in the United States struggle with an excess of freedom, however, many other countries in the world, including especially the former Marxist countries, suffer the opposite problem. An excess of order and the need for individual freedom has in those countries pent up a passion for freedom and democracy that, unleashed, is now sweeping the world. Self-governance is vital to solving the problems of these countries as well.

Until the integration between freedom and order is accomplished, politics will remain in crisis—a form of war (to paraphrase Clausewitz) carried on by other means. Until the integration is accomplished, conservatives will continue to see the freedom left, represented by the ACLU and the counterculture, as carriers (respectively) of moral relativism and nihilism, and the order left (heirs of the socialist tradition) as authoritarians. And liberals will continue to see the freedom right (libertarians) as exponents of greed, and the order right (traditionalists) as authoritarians.

The reality is that each view is correct but incomplete; all these factions await the integration that still eludes us.

The problem is in the loss of agreement about personal obligation, all concepts of which remain based on tradition. In Hamilton's time, and in Manchester's, there was widespread consensus about order and obligation. When there is agreement about personal responsibilities—about what people's "true interests" are—the problem of integrating freedom and obligation is relatively small. But when obligations are unclear, as they have become with the decline of tradition, integrating freedom and order becomes extremely difficult.

One thing is clear. Integration of freedom and order—or individualism and community—depends on belief in the self-governing capacities of all human beings. It depends on the belief that the principal venue of moral improvement is local—individuals and their local communities, participating in and working through various levels of government. This is true no matter what role is ultimately conceived for the central state. Unless the underlying values of a society are healthy (that is, with freedom and order integrated), those who administer government policies will pursue their own, rather than public, ends. Moreover, if people do not live by their responsibilities to treat each other with dignity and respect, government policies will be forced to operate in a hostile environment that will relentlessly undermine any good they may do.

The need for healthy values highlights a major difficulty we must overcome. That difficulty resides in the fact that our entire debate on issues of freedom and order centers on politics—especially the politics of central governments. Thus it speaks only to centralized entities, almost never to private or decentralized action and values. There will be no hope of accomplishing the synthesis of freedom and order we seek unless we stop vesting all hope in centralized public action. There will be no hope until we move beyond traditional politics and broaden our concern about values to include the realm of the private and the local.

The latter conclusion will be as difficult for the left to accept as for the right. For liberals are determined to use the state to secure social justice and equality just as many conservatives are committed to using it to oppose abortion and regulate other aspects of private moral life. Nevertheless, there are good reasons for believing that serious social campaigns, be they against abortion and drugs or in favor of social justice and equality, will not be possible until we stop relying on government policies as the almost exclusive instruments to pursue them.

Moving beyond Politics

In most places and for centuries, the debate about freedom and order has centered on individual freedom and rights to protect individuals from the power of the state, concerns analogous to those of adolescents seeking to be free from their parents' values. In the Western democracies, as I have noted, a competing concept of liberty appeared at the end of the nineteenth century, together with a new theory of rights for the disadvantaged. These new concepts (their advocates argued) required the active support of government. Therefore, the debate in the Western democracies has pitted libertarians, such as Milton Friedman, Friedrich A. Hayek, and Frank Knight, advocating negative freedom (the older concept of freedom from constraint by the state), against liberal and progressive reformers advocating government actions that expand opportunities and therefore the effective freedoms enjoyed by disadvantaged groups. In the end, however, neither side has a really positive notion of freedom; they are arguing over different views of negative freedom: freedom *from* government interference versus freedom *from* want. Both views are concerned only with removing external impediments to freedom, defined differently. This traditional debate (which is still with us) has no positive vision of freedom and therefore no basis from which to imagine integration of freedom and order. It is concerned only with how the political order should balance, rather than integrate, the two values. It sees only a zero-sum game, in which more of one value automatically means less of the other.

Integrating the two ideas is possible because we need and demand both. We demand freedom, and we also seek and need purpose, meaning, and connections beyond ourselves. Freedom is an instrument, satisfying the need of modern individuals to live conscious lives, lives not driven by habit alone. Recall that in the positive sense of freedom as consciousness, freedom is an instrument that releases a person from tradition and compels a search for new terms of order. In this perspective, people can have both freedom *and* order: in fact, they *must* have both because they *need* both.

Integrating freedom and order is possible only if we move beyond our preoccupation with negative freedom (freedom from tradition) and search actively for new sources of authority and values—values that respond to our need for choice and for conscious engagement in moral life. Such new values would be personal because they would be individually affirmed; but in giving purpose, meaning, and connection beyond ourselves, they would also define the individual's obligation to his society. Integrating freedom and order would thus allow us to have the left's commitment to social justice *and* the libertarians' to individual freedom.

To address the problem of integration seriously, however, the discussion must move beyond traditional politics and consider deeper issues. Specifically, it must consider the question of how and in what personal and political circumstances people would freely choose to be obligated. Under what conditions would they choose order and responsibility? And what would be the nature of the order they would choose? These questions apply not only to individuals relating privately to one another, but also to them as citizens, participating through institutions in the public life of the larger community and state.

Since freedom and consciousness pose problems for individuals, we cannot avoid considering certain social and psychological issues that focus on individuals. These include understanding, first, *why* people increasingly demand freedom and reject traditional morals, and second, understanding *how* individuals, consciously working in and through freedom, might establish the sense of purpose and connection beyond themselves. These issues are important in considering the search for obligation and responsibility in both private and public life.

Society's need to move away from traditional politics to a politics informed and animated by psychology (perhaps of a new kind) reflects the crucial role that conscious individuals will need to play in this process. The new politics must encourage self-knowledge and allow people to find purpose and meaning by making commitments and reaching beyond themselves. The crucial political point, however, is that much of this process must take place outside and beyond the realm of central governments. It must be focused on the search for new, self-governing institutions at the local level that engage individual citizens to work for common purposes.

In the next two chapters, I will look more closely at how the tension between freedom and order is an important reality—perhaps the most important reality—underlying the positions of both the right and the left. Until the tension is resolved and the concepts are meaningfully integrated, it will remain very hard to know just what modern conservatism and liberalism are—or what they might be.

2

Conservatives Return to Freedom

In the opening pages of his 1970 anthology of twentieth-century American conservative thought, *Did You Ever See a Dream Walking?* William F. Buckley, Jr., acknowledges the difficulty of saying just what modern American conservatism is.[1] When people insist on precision, he says, the closest he comes is to quote Richard Weaver's humorous definition: "the paradigm of essences toward which the phenomenology of the world is in continuing approximation." Nevertheless, Buckley feels he knows "if not what conservatism is, at least who a conservative is."

Confronted with the difficulty of analyzing a term we all use so freely, one might ask, Why bother? Why should anyone worry about producing a definition of conservatism, or liberalism for that matter? Why can't we just be satisfied with multiple definitions, even if they sometimes conflict? The answer is that the coherence of our political discourse depends on it. As long as the principal words in our political debate seem to mean conflicting things, it will not be coherent. Moreover, even if our political debate seems entirely driven by the tensions among apparently different groupings—freedom and order conservatives, and freedom and order liberals—none of them understand their *own* positions as exclusively advocating either freedom or order. Nearly everyone believes that his or her position incorporates both values. The reason for such wishfulness is sound: because we instinctively understand that each value is incomplete without the other. Few would want to advocate either value alone, for fear of seeming extreme. But the philosophical differences between, say, Milton Friedman and the Moral Majority indicate that conservatism has not incorporated these values equally.

The unresolved conflict explains why few conservatives hazard comprehensive theories of their beliefs. A few intrepid souls, including Buckley, the late Frank Meyer, and to some degree the neoconservatives, have tried to embrace both freedom and order positions, though not to venture a systematic definition of conservatism that accommodates both. Many others have given up: commentators as varied as Russell Kirk, the late Clinton Rossiter, and George F. Will, among others, have argued that only advocates of traditional order deserve to be called conservatives. Many libertarians, including Friedman, agree: they disavow the label and insist they are liberals.

The trouble is that discounting the freedom, or libertarian, side has the effect of excluding many—I would argue most—prominent conservatives. Such a definition, for example, makes it impossible to say the Reagan administration was conservative; for if we exclude free-market economics from conservatism, President Reagan forfeited his conservative mantle the moment he made economics rather than social issues like abortion and school prayer the centerpiece of his administration. It is hard to see how excluding libertarian economists would clarify dialogue, because doing so would alter fundamentally our common understanding of who is conservative. No matter how confused it may be, our general assumption is that free-market libertarians are every bit as conservative as traditional conservatives. But our precise understanding at any moment depends very much on context and circumstances. To an opponent, "conservative" can mean either "obsessed by morality and order and indifferent to freedom," or "obsessed by personal freedom and indifferent to social values."

Despite the seeming incoherence, modern conservatism as practiced by its major political exponents—especially Ronald Reagan in the United States and Margaret Thatcher in Great Britain—embraces freedom as its "superior function" (to borrow Jung's phrase for dominant tendency) and serves order and morality primarily by exhortation. This is clear from the extent to which both Reagan and Thatcher emphasized economics rather than social issues.

Modern liberals, on the other hand, have come to focus primarily on policies to strengthen order (community, equality, etc.), paying homage to freedom mainly in their personal antagonism to the traditional moral and political order.

In this chapter, I will review how modern conservatism came to change places with the left, taking over the left's historical emphasis on freedom and yielding its emphasis on order. In exploring how these superior functions manifest themselves in today's politics, I will argue that the conflict between libertarians and traditional conservatives does not go nearly as deep as people on both sides of the divide commonly assume. In the end, even traditional conservatives will return to modern conservatism's primary value, which is freedom. And the converse is true of both the freedom and order left: they will ultimately return to their superior function: order.

One fundamental point remains concerning all of these positions, however: Americans, both conservatives and liberals, and increasing numbers of people in other countries, see themselves as committed to both freedom *and* order. In practical terms, this means (for instance) that whenever a presidential administration places substantial emphasis on either value—freedom or order— it will produce a dialectical reaction from the advocates of the other, even within the governing political party. President Reagan's emphasis on economic freedom thus engendered President Bush's call for a "kinder, gentler" nation. And when Bush ignored the traditional right during his presidential term, partisans of "family values" reacted by seizing control of the 1992 Republican convention.

A similar reaction occurred on the left during the 1960s, when the Kennedy-Johnson administrations' emphasis on massive social and political projects—epitomized in the phrases "New Frontier" and "Great Society"—was rejected by the New Left (the freedom left), which demanded decentralization and attacked all large-scale organizations, both public and private.

To understand how we got to our present understanding of left and right, we must begin by recalling how the roles of left and right have changed in the course of the advance of freedom through history.

Left and Right Change Places

The human experience began in both order and disorder. In the face of enormous physical (external) disorder, man's preconscious social and psychological (internal) world was extremely ordered, and was sustained by habit. Over the millennia, conditions in both realms shifted: as science allowed man increasingly to control the external world and bring order to it, his internal world grew ever more disordered. Growing demands for freedom have by now all but destroyed the old (social and psychological) order in our society, and in its place is the disorder we observe in the crisis of values and in our politics.

Freedom has thus moved across history in two distinct phases, first pushing traditional societies toward modernization and democracy, and second pushing post-traditional societies to search for a new form of order, consistent with individualism. The second phase animates the effort to integrate freedom and order.

In the first phase, when traditional societies move toward freedom—again, adolescence is a useful metaphor—the political right stands for religious and political order against the left's push for freedom and democracy. In most countries in the world this continues to be the case—even in countries that are nominally socialist. In the former Soviet Union, for example, proponents of *glasnost* described defenders of the traditional political and moral order as "conservative" even though that order was socialist, or "leftist." The result of such relativism is often terrible confusion. Here, for example, are the *Washington Post*'s remarks on struggles in the Hungarian Communist party a few years ago:

> The final list of presidium members made clear that no well-known *conservatives,* such as . . . Karoly Grosz or . . . Janos Bercz, would have a leadership role in the new party. Both of these men have suggested that they will form a *far-left* Communist Party.[2]

"Conservatives" are invariably taken to favor order, as long as it is not perceived to be of an actively revolutionary kind. In this sense, newly formed revolutionary governments cannot be conservative; they only become conservative when they have been in power long enough to behave like monopoly capitalists (as almost all Marxist regimes now have).

A second phase becomes evident in post-traditional societies such as the United States, when there is no traditional order remaining for conservatives to embrace. Now the relation between left and right begins to shift in two important ways. Conservatives emphasize freedom, and liberals and the left focus their energy on building a post-traditional political order (community, equality); yet both sides in fact now embrace both freedom and order in an effort to integrate them.

In observing the conflict within these positions, one may note the recent emergence of some extraordinary experiments among conservatives, exploring different approaches to the integration of freedom and order. All are concrete, specific political and intellectual programs of action, in the United States and other countries. All of these programs, which I will explore later in the book, have stimulated impressive support from people on the left, which reveals how surprisingly thin is the line between left and right.

A Muted Conflict

The relationship between freedom and order conservatives is not simply one of conflict; their disputes also reflect a dialectical process of searching for a way to integrate the two values.

Conflict among conservatives rarely breaks into open political debate. It simmers just underground and tends to appear especially when conservatives hold political power. When it becomes overt, however, all sense of rationality tends to collapse. An example of this happened during a formal debate in the late 1970s between traditional conservative Paul Weyrich and me. The debate, on the subject of rape, was held at a meeting of intellectual conservatives organized by the Philadelphia Society. In my remarks, addressed to both traditional and libertarian conservatives, my emphasis on freedom so agitated my opponent that he accused me of being indifferent to morality and thus without a basis from which to oppose rape. I argued that an atmosphere of freedom was necessary to define the moral content of all behavior—that without freedom morality was impossible. From the audience Milton Friedman responded with rare and passionate anger to the effect that my opponent's comment was so far outside the pale of civilized discourse that he should never again be invited as a speaker.

The truly remarkable thing about the debate, however, was that it took place at all. Traditional conservatives and libertarians often express bitter hostility toward each other, but rarely in each others' company. Nobody debates, because bitterness tends to overwhelm any value in the exchange.

Especially in the early part of President Reagan's first term, issues such as the draft, school prayer, and abortion caused bitter conflict between traditional and libertarian conservatives. Even during the transition period following President Reagan's election in 1980, New Right leaders such as Howard Phillips were saying that they had been sold out—that the president-elect had turned his back on social issues. This charge recalled similar bitterness in conflicts between the New Left and the old over analogous issues of freedom and order when the left held power during the Kennedy-Johnson years. And it was echoed again later, as libertarians looked with horror on the 1992 Republican party platform and convention, which were dominated by the religious right.

Such conflict, when it occurs, between traditional conservatives and libertarians makes it hard to see the extraordinary agreement that normally exists between them. Adam Meyerson, editor of the Heritage Foundation journal *Policy Review,* provided—I assume unwittingly—an extraordinary opportunity to observe that agreement in the summer of 1984, when the journal sponsored a debate on "Sex and God in American Politics." On one side he had staunch libertarians such as Milton Friedman, and on the other traditionalists including Irving Kristol and, from the New Right, Paul Weyrich and Moral Majority leader Jerry Falwell. I am sure that Meyerson set out to give his readers some real fireworks. Nevertheless, even on the social issues such as the draft, abortion, drugs, and anything to do with sex—issues assumed to generate the greatest conflict between libertarians and traditional conservatives—the "debate" was so placid and boring that it was good only to induce sleep. Everyone, including both Weyrich and Falwell, embraced freedom as his primary value. On homosexuality, for instance, Friedman said, "I don't think it is any business of the government, so long as it is purely voluntary." Falwell replied: "I personally believe that homosexuals should be afforded total civil rights like all other Americans . . . [including] equal access to housing accommodations and job opportunities. . . ." And New Right leader Weyrich affirmed a basic libertarian commitment: "I don't think it is the business of the government," he said, "to tell people what they can and cannot do."

My own experience confirms this fundamental agreement. Although most conservatives appear at first glance to argue narrowly and exclusively in favor of one idea or the other, for either freedom or order, a closer look will show that they also embrace the opposite idea as well. Traditional conservatives emphasize freedom from government interference as their primary value, as Falwell and Weyrich did—especially when, as in education issues, the right to impart values to one's own children appears threatened. And libertarians acknowledge the importance of personal order and structure. Milton Friedman stated this with special force when he said that the great problem threatening our civilization was "the decline of both personal and social responsibility."[3]

The Dilemma of the Neoconservatives

The neoconservatives joined the conservative movement from the ranks of the anticommunist left at the end of the 1960s, during the breakdown of the political and moral order that happened at that time. They, like other conservatives, are defenders of traditional values, which in our society means bourgeois values and our "commercial civilization." They defend the nonheroic lives of ordinary people. Their appeals are to virtue and order, looking toward the traditional conservative vision more than to ideals of freedom. But they are also interested in something they call "democratic capitalism," and a number of the neoconservatives were major exponents and theoreticians of Ronald Reagan's supply-side economics.

Neoconservatives are deeply concerned about the dependence of liberal democracy on the spiritual and moral standards of traditional authority, especially traditional religion. For them our crisis of values is a logical consequence of the long decline of authority, and they vest their hope in education to reconstruct a moral and spiritual foundation for our free institutions. Their commitment to education is specifically to traditional education, reflecting their belief (following Aristotle) that people can be habituated to virtue. The idea is that if you teach people to be good, the act of being good will provide its own lesson, and they will learn to be good.

This position raises a fundamental problem, one that torments both the left and the right. It is the conflict in our politics between the political and the personal, between idea and experience.

The first rule in teaching values is that the teachers must live by the values they espouse. Neoconservative intellectuals, however, are modern people. More than that, they are an intellectual elite. They "think a lot." They introspect. In short, they are individualists. They do not themselves live by habit; they cannot. Like all modern people with intense consciousness of their individual selves, they are driven to understand and make conscious commitments to values. Even if they live by traditional values, they do so not because they are traditional, but because they have made a conscious choice.

Because of who they are, neoconservatives must, therefore, live with at least apparent conflicts between the political and cultural positions they hold on the one hand, and their own behavior on the other. For instance, neoconservative women condemn the women's movement, but all of them are themselves independent and success-ful—good examples of much that the women's movement stands for. For example, the "godmother" of the neoconservatives, Ger-trude Himmelfarb, is a leading scholar, an authority on Victorian England. Midge Decter, a major critic of feminism, is a prominent and brilliant writer and speaker. Neoconservatives also affirm the importance of religion in society, often without being themselves religious (or at least actively so). I once heard Owen Harries, coedi-tor of *The National Interest,* affirm the importance of religion and then confess he was an atheist. Irving Kristol and Gertrude Himmel-farb, on the other hand, like to say that they are "nonobservant Orthodox Jews." Finally, like many intellectuals, neoconservatives tend to live in cities. Although they defend the values associated with the countryside and with rural life in general, they could not them-selves assume the very traditional life-style that they defend intellec-tually. Many of them have lived at least part of their lives in New York City, that most urban of cities, because it stimulates them, keeps them "moving." The static quality of rural life, like the static nature of traditional values themselves, may offer the ideal prescrip-tion for political and social stability; but it simply cannot serve the emotional and existential needs of most intellectuals, left or right— no matter what values they espouse.

Since most do not, themselves, live by traditional values, conser-vative intellectuals cannot claim that those values "work" for people who, like themselves, cannot live bound by tradition. Therefore, despite their commitment to traditional education and to learning and living through custom, the neoconservatives have no choice but exempt themselves from their own prescriptions. This leaves them nothing positive to say to people estranged from traditional values, who make up a growing portion of our increasingly educated population. For such people, the neoconservatives' role is only negative: resisting the intellectual left, criticizing excesses of freedom and the decline of traditional values. Neoconservatives have nothing to say to the intellectual left because they share the left's problem. Most of them have made no strong, positive, personal affirmation of conservative values.

The neoconservatives' concern about tradition and order is important. The great threat to free institutions lies in the possibility that the search for new forms of authority and values will fail, and that people will end up demanding that order be imposed on them, as many of the most educated did during the 1960s. They did this when they embraced the full program of the order left, which, through statements like the Kerner Commission's report on urban race riots, called in essence for a social revolution led by the federal government. Radical demands for an imposition of order, though in a more military form, are now the principal threat to the newly independent republics of the former Soviet Union. People will not tolerate chaos and anarchy indefinitely; at some point they will demand that authority, even the military, step in and restore order.

While traditional conservatives (including the neoconservatives) are effective in warning about the dangers we face if we do not rediscover strong sources of order and values, they have no remedy for the problem except a return to traditional authority. They are limited to renewed appeals to faith and virtue, the same approach adopted by less sophisticated people. Such an appeal may work for ordinary working people, but they are not the problem. Traditional authority does nothing to convince intellectuals and highly educated people, including intellectual conservatives. In fact, society has changed so much in the past twenty-five years that one cannot even be so sure about "ordinary people": there is considerable evidence that tradition and habit have an ever weaker hold on them as well.

But the situation for intellectuals is very clear. Because they feel so intense a need to understand values and to feel a sense of active participation in consenting to them, appeals to the old virtues and authorities, including faith, often provoke only resistance in them.

In their failure to address the increasingly common need to understand and "choose" values as the price of consent, conservatives make a fundamental mistake in their judgment of the nature of man. The continuing importance of subjective consciousness—advancing in the species as it does in each individual at adolescence—explains why tradition has lost so much of its staying power, at least in the advanced industrial countries of the West. However difficult individual choice is, the erosion of authority based on faith is quickly ushering in the time when individual choice, responsive to the evidence of experience, will be the only authority left.

To avoid misunderstanding, I must insert an important caution here. I am not saying that values are true simply because people choose them. The point I am arguing assumes the truth of certain values, independent of whether people commit to them. My point is that, increasingly, people will refuse to commit to any values unless they can participate in the search to understand and make voluntary commitment to them. And part of defining truth is the need of modern people for conscious engagement in moral life. Life based on habit provides no purpose or meaning for a conscious person; only conscious engagement can do that. This is so as it regards both personal and political values.

If conservatives fail to appreciate the advancing need to examine values, it is because they do not take individualism seriously. In this, of course, they are not alone. In different ways, most intellectual traditions avoid the issue of individualism. Even libertarians, who spend their lives celebrating individual freedom and choice, in their own way avoid the real issue.

"The deeper one explores into the self, without any transcendental frame of reference," Irving Kristol has written, "the clearer it becomes that nothing is there."[4] True enough, the self is elusive. The transcendental yearning of those who hold nontraditional, individualistic values has become painfully evident since the New Left's appearance in the early 1960s. The question is, how does an individual reach the transcendent? How, in an age of *intellectual* consciousness, consciousness of the mind alone, does one regain touch with the soul? How can we integrate subjectivity and objectivity?

I will later explore the rising interest in things spiritual among cultural descendants of the New Left. The point here is that the need and longing to transcend the self, to feel connected to things outside, to the whole, is undeniable. This need is especially evident among adherents of the environmentalist movement, which is every day gaining strength. The feeling of connectedness is what has been lost in society's increasing intellectual preoccupation with analyzing reality, with reducing it to ever smaller, discrete parts. But restored contact with the transcendent is not possible any longer through blind faith. Increasing consciousness of the self requires something more active—a greater sense of participation in the process. It also requires guidance from "teachers" who are sensitive to the special needs of our increasingly educated and individualistic population.

The Dilemma of the Libertarians

Libertarians are the political group most explicit in embracing individualism and free choice. Their entire social and political program is based on a desire to maximize free choice. However, they too avoid the real issue of individualism.

If traditional conservatives cannot propound a vision of order that includes freedom, libertarians are preoccupied only with freedom; they have no serious vision of order. They focus solely on the external conditions of freedom, for they take freedom to be man's natural condition and assume that everyone else feels the same unqualified desire for it. From this they conclude that people who lack their enthusiasm must lack "the facts." And so they spend their energies writing "objective" arguments for unrestrained freedom, which they imagine will put their opponents right.

Libertarians tend to be astonished that the most "modern" people, the most educated and the young, are rarely persuaded by their arguments—are rarely interested in "the facts"—and often choose to sacrifice freedom for political institutions that impose order and virtue. Most people, however, want more than freedom; they want (because they need) purpose and meaning, a vision of the good life—a vision of what to do with their freedom. This is especially true of people who are estranged and alienated from the traditional sources of meaning.

Dostoyevsky's legend of the Grand Inquisitor symbolized the truth that intellectuals, no matter what they say, are greatly ambivalent about freedom; since they are so anxious about freedom for themselves, they can't tolerate it for others. Friedrich A. Hayek, although he was a libertarian, reaffirmed freedom's reliance on order in *The Constitution of Liberty:* "It is probably true," he wrote, "that a successful free society will always in a large measure be a tradition-bound society."[5] And Edmund Burke, a traditionalist, made the same point in his famous statement that "Society cannot exist, unless a controlling power upon will and appetite be placed somewhere; and the less of it there is within, the more there must be without."[6] In the absence of order, that is, whether intrinsic or imposed, there can be neither society nor freedom.

These arguments, made by three very different thinkers, affirm the central truth about the dependence of freedom on order. This truth allows us to understand how support for freedom has deteriorated in the West over the last century—despite the perception, widely held, that it has grown exponentially.

The deterioration has occurred because of the decline of traditional forms of authority and community, especially religion. These traditional forms afforded the social and psychological protection that enabled people to enjoy their freedom and invested them with a passionate attachment to it. Nothing was more natural for them than freedom, within accepted bounds, and their commitment to it was beyond question. This acceptance of the dependence of freedom on order explains why Adam Smith, the father of modern economics, could have written both *The Wealth of Nations* (supporting freedom) and *The Theory of Moral Sentiments* (supporting order).

In the thirty-plus years since 1960, traditional authority and values have accelerated their decline. Demands for freedom of personal expression have replaced the commitments to duty and responsibility that defined the lives of most people in the 1950s and before. This change is responsible for the phenomenon at the heart of the *psychological* problem of integrating freedom and order—the longing for a subjectively validated order, both personal and political.

This longing continues; yet no solution to the alienation and personal "separateness" characteristic of modernity is in sight. The value of order introduced from without will continue to decline. All attempts to objectify and externalize values and morality, whether in traditional religions or in traditional Marxism or contemporary welfare state (order) liberalism, will therefore decline with it. The effect of this process is as evident in the former Eastern bloc countries as in the Western democracies. Nevertheless, as this process of decline continues, the longing for a new order sustains the impulse (evident in many parts of our politics) to impose one politically.

Although traditional conservatives have been correct that the decline of social authority—family, church, and local community—

would undermine the social and psychological foundations of liberal democracy, they stumbled in their diagnosis of the problem and therefore failed to prescribe a workable solution. They reason for this is that they did not take individualism seriously. Libertarians, on the other hand, failed to see the need for order to complement their emphasis on individualism. They focused exclusively on the external conditions of freedom and democracy, confining their concern to politics. For them, it was enough that government interfere less in the private lives of citizens. Unfortunately, focusing on the external architecture of freedom avoids the really difficult conditions that we must face to resolve the problem of freedom and order.

The libertarian's dilemma becomes clear when we consider that many of them insist on being called "classical liberals," as they are still referred to in Europe, rather than conservatives. They are right to make the distinction because their focus is on individual freedom, not moral and social order (which conservatives historically have emphasized). But the problem of freedom today is so different—or at least more complex—than it was in the nineteenth century, that the question arises of whether it means very much to be a nineteenth-century liberal in the late twentieth-century world.

Their failure to deal with moral and social values encourages the conclusion that libertarians, whose favorite institution is capitalism, are inherently materialistic. The misapprehension is not made only of libertarians; it applies also (for the most part) to free-market economists, who appeal constantly to self-interest. "If there is one thing you can trust people to do," the libertarian economist Armen Alchian once remarked to me, "it is to put their interest ahead of yours." The cynicism is amusing, but it serves the ideals of capitalism and freedom badly.

Libertarian conservatives can be idealistic, often explicitly so, though many of them choose not to be. Instead of celebrating the highest aspirations and impulses of the human spirit, some libertarians even go so far as to extol the lowest. Ayn Rand's celebration of selfishness is the most obvious example of this.*

Praising selfishness serves capitalism as badly as does the

---

*It is interesting, nevertheless, that even Rand may have meant by "selfishness" something very different from the common understanding of that word. For her novels do not celebrate people who are merely egotistical; in offering heroes such as Howard Roark *(The Fountainhead)*, they celebrate idealists.

neoconservative's standard defense of our "commercial civilization."
Both cynicism and "realism," in different ways, distort the cause of
capitalism and freedom by giving the impression that idealism plays
no part in capitalism—nor indeed in any free system. From this, it
becomes easy to understand why many people conclude that if you
are idealistic, you have to be a socialist.

When conservatives of either type, libertarian or traditionalist,
aim their appeal at this harsh sort of "realism," they give up any
chance of influencing or persuading their principal adversaries, that
is, most intellectuals. The reason for this is that intellectuals and the
people who identify with them—the opinion-making classes,
broadly understood—think in an idiom of idealism, which often
means socialism. It may even be irrelevant to such people that
socialism does not work, that it has not produced either wealth or
equality anywhere it has been tried. Whoever said that being idealistic—striving for higher values—would be easy? Thus, socialists
paraphrase G. K. Chesterton's famous remark about Christianity:
socialism—they say—has not been tried and found wanting; it has
been found difficult and not tried. The left searches for new sources
of authority and values in appeals to idealism—appeals to the
heights of human possibility—because such appeals express what
people on the left seek personally for themselves. Intellectuals of the
left will simply not hear arguments unless they are cast in idealistic
terms. And the reason for this is that ideals call upon individuals to
lead conscious, moral lives and not simply to follow traditions
blindly.

Again, the challenge is both personal and political. Until recently, libertarians have missed enormous opportunities to reach out
to the intellectual left and attract recruits to their political banner.
The truth that libertarians have failed to convey is that they stake
their success on hopes that free people will choose the good. There
is no higher idealism.

The New Conservative Idealism

If conservatives have in the past not been good at evoking a positive
vision of political idealism, there are signs that this may be changing. In fact, as Marxism's idealistic pretensions have everywhere
been exposed, new conservative idealisms are appearing in places

as disparate as South Africa, Peru, and California. All are propounded by libertarian conservatives who are rallying coalitions that defy the traditional left-right spectrum.

These experiments have several things in common. First, these new idealists believe in the potential of individuals and reject the beliefs of both left and right that anyone, especially the disadvantaged, must somehow either depend on, or must be subservient to, larger social institutions. This is true with regard to both the left's desire to replace "exploitive" traditional hierarchies and capitalism by government institutions and planning, and the right's belief that only traditional institutions can give people, including the poor, a sense of purpose and belonging. These new idealists believe in the self-governing capacities of people, and they hold that the primary obstacle to full participation by the world's poor in the economic and social life of their countries is the commitment to collectivism held by both the left and important elements on the right.

The most dramatic example of this new thinking has been the extraordinary advocacy of the "informal sector" (the underground economy or "gray" market) by Hernando de Soto and his Instituto Libertad y Democracia (ILD) in Lima, Peru. In his best-selling book, *El Otro Sendero* (The Other Path), de Soto argues that, in Peru and other Latin American countries, immense social injustice exists in the effective economic exclusion of large numbers of the poorest people, who are forced by the cost of compliance with bureaucratic regulations to work illegally, "off-the-books," forgoing benefit of legal and economic institutions. The enormity of these crippling costs is suggested by a simulation that the ILD conducted, an attempt to gain formal recognition of a small garment business owning two sewing machines. Negotiating the tortuous Peruvian business licensing process required 289 days. By comparison, a similar process, conducted in Tampa, Florida, took 4 hours. Although wealthy Peruvians can overcome these hurdles by hiring expensive legal help, the poor, primarily comprising Indians and mestizos, cannot. Impediments like these suggest why in Lima the "informals" control 93 percent of public transport, 43 percent of the housing industry, and 35 percent of the textile industry.

De Soto's analysis turns traditional political idioms, labels, and categories on their heads. For rather than posit a battle between "socialism" and "capitalism," he describes a clash of vested interests, including on the one hand both traditional oligarchies and socialist bureaucrats, and on the other entrepreneurial poor people and minority-group members, who maintain vibrant capitalist economies in the face of incredible difficulties. The size of the informal economy is therefore quite extraordinary: 60 percent of person-days in Peru are now worked in the informal sector; informal enterprises produce about 40 percent of the reported output of the nation without the benefit of legally enforceable contracts, secure property rights, and other economic and legal institutions necessary to realize economies of scale. In a study of five other countries, Mohamed Salahdine and I found even more extreme situations in Asia and North Africa.[7]

Under these circumstances, it becomes easy to see why Marxism became a symbol largely without content—a banner behind which those outraged by injustice attacked capitalists and the capitalist West. Having cut through the mythology to the reality of economic and social relations, de Soto's free-market, libertarian proposals for wholesale deregulation of Peru's economy was endorsed by both the conservative and Marxist candidates for president in that politically polarized country's 1990 election.

It would be beyond the scope of this book to do justice here to the similar programs now spreading throughout the world that draw on the same basic idealism and belief in human capacities for self-governance. Some examples, however, include Leon Louw and Frances Kendall's work with black entrepreneurs and local community groups in South Africa to broaden property rights, Mohamed Salahdine's work in creating new empowerment models for social welfare programs in Morocco, the work of the Center for Self-Governance in San Francisco in transforming low-income housing projects and schools, and countless similar projects throughout the former Eastern bloc.

These initiatives include some that do not identify themselves as conservative. Neither the path-breaking San Francisco drug rehabilitation program, the Delancey Street Foundation, and its imitators in other cities, nor the Grameen Bank in Bangladesh and similar banks serving the informal sector in other developing countries are considered to be conservative. Yet they and many other programs like them are operated along the lines discussed here—in sharp contrast to the quasi-socialist public assistance programs operated by governments. Whatever ideological labels happen to be attached to them, they are all committed to "empowering people"; wherever they can be found, "conservatives" and "liberals" are working together to build a better future.

In all of these situations and others, people in every socioeconomic, ethnic, racial, and religious group are working to integrate individual freedom and community order. The energy of their initiatives allows them to overcome attempts to oppose them, whether from the socialist left or the oligarchic right. In many places, these essentially conservative idealists are recruiting to their causes support from people on the left—especially people committed to the decentralizing ideas advanced by the New Left during the 1960s. Community leaders and activists of all sorts have become their colleagues, and the unlikely alliances they have built are attracting the notice of journalists looking for inventive attempts to remold society.

One important indicator of our political crisis is that although these programs are celebrated across the political spectrum, few candidates for office have drawn on them for lessons that might be more generally applied. Instead, these programs are seen as unique, separate—not concerning the rest of us. This reluctance to learn from success only shows how calcified are the traditional modes of our political behavior and thought.

In the final hours of the twentieth century, upheavals in Marxist countries everywhere have put the traditional left on the defensive to an extraordinary degree. A friend of mine with impeccable connections to the activist left recently expressed exasperation with conservatives' reluctance to recognize the extent of their triumph. "Why," he asked, "don't conservatives just proclaim their victory and stop complaining?" The reason they do not lies in their recognition that, although collectivist government answers may have failed, Alexander Hamilton's challenge—for societies freely to choose their obligations—still remains. The problem of freedom and order is still with us. Although Marx misdiagnosed the nature of the modern dilemma (attributing it to class struggle), the problems he saw in industrial capitalism remain very serious, even as they have turned out to be even more serious in industrialized *socialist* countries.

But the left continues to have much to contribute to the integration of freedom and order, and it is to the recent history of the left's search that I now turn.

3

Liberals Opt for Order

If the right suffers severe problems, the left is in full-blown crisis. The left's dilemma, like the right's, lies in the apparent contradiction between its freedom and order tendencies. One tendency—the order left—looks to politics, especially centralized politics, to realize its visions of community and equality. The order left dominates the Democratic party in the United States because its principal constituent interest groups are of the order left. These include labor unions, environmentalist organizations, the women's movement—all of them committed to using the federal government to realize political, economic, and social objectives.

The other tendency—the freedom left—emphasizes individual rights *against* the traditional political and moral order and, especially in the counterculture, celebrates extreme, individualistic behavior. This position is most evident in civil liberties organizations such as the ACLU, in *avant-garde* art circles, and among the clientele of counterculture institutions such as coffeehouses. It is also prominent in entertainment, such as movies showing government officials pursuing sinister ends with savage indifference to citizens' rights. Oliver Stone is the most prominent filmmaker of this school, as he demonstrated most recently in *JFK*, his movie about President Kennedy's assassination.

The order left emphasizes obligations and responsibilities; the freedom left focuses on freedom from responsibilities—at least in their traditional form. One group looks toward politics, and especially centralized government; the other looks away from politics to other arenas of life, while actively encouraging citizens at every turn to distrust their government. Most people on the order left, finally, are committed to using reason, science, and the forces of material "progress" as a means of helping and defending ordinary working people. The freedom left rejects traditional bourgeois values, is highly suspicious of science, actively opposes progress, and often celebrates intuition and feeling over reason.

The conflict between these positions explains why coherent left-liberal government has become impossible. Until a way is found to integrate the freedom and order tendencies in a single vision, the order left will continue trying to use central government power to impose its programs on people—which is all it knows how to do. If it succeeds, it will provoke an inevitable reaction not only from the right, but from the freedom left, which seeks to be free from imposed order.

When such a reaction occurs, the order left in power is newly perceived as "conservative," as fighting to maintain the status quo against challenges from the freedom left. This is what has recently happened in the former Soviet Union, China, and the East European countries. There the new "left" celebrates freedom wrested from the old order—even though that order was or still is socialist—and the "right" supports restoration of socialist order.

Although socialism and Marxism have declined as potent ideas throughout the world, milder commitments to use the central state to achieve social justice remain the shibboleth of the order left everywhere. Even these qualified commitments can provoke reactions, however. In fact, one such reaction occurred after Americans elected a president dedicated to an openly liberal agenda in 1960. John F. Kennedy took office with grand, idealistic designs not only for the nation, but for the world. When he said in his inaugural address that "we shall pay any price, bear any burden, meet any hardship, support any friend, oppose any foe to assure the survival and success of liberty," he was expressing very eloquently the larger designs of the order left. The New Frontier program, which his campaign promised would get the country "moving again," was to be engineered by the federal government. This provided a strong rallying cry for the order left. A reaction developed, however, in the year following Kennedy's inauguration. In 1962 the freedom left produced the Port Huron Statement announcing the formation of the Students for a Democratic Society. The Port Huron Statement marked the beginning of the New Left as a prominent political movement. Rachel Carson's *Silent Spring,* published in the same year, initiated the modern environmentalist movement, which rejected the order left's central commitments to reason, science, and material progress.

From Order Right to Freedom Left

It is interesting to consider how the freedom and order lefts relate to their counterpart positions on the right. One can see in their evolution a struggle to integrate freedom and order, as the left and right, in different periods, emphasized first one ideal, then the other, trying to find the right balance between the two. That they have not succeeded in finding a balance is because they cannot: the issue is not balance, but integration.

In dialectical (and hugely oversimplified) sequence, one may construct an historical progression beginning at the time of the American and French revolutions. Holding power at the beginning of the sequence was the order right, which represented then as today the traditional moral and political order. The decline of this *ancien régime* engendered the rationalist, modernist response of the classical eighteenth- and nineteenth-century liberals, who celebrated the individual and who eventually became what is now the freedom right. Then came another response, from nineteenth-century radicals and socialists, who sought a new rationalist order, and whose descendants are the social democratic, or order, left. Finally came the freedom left, the nineteenth-century Romantics, who returned to an emphasis on the individual. Today we find the counterculture descendants of the Romantics celebrating feeling and spirituality, suspicious of scientific progress, and seeking community and belonging in radically decentralized ways.

It is probably inevitable that the rationalist positions on both the left and right—the freedom right (libertarians) and order left (social democrats)—are the most political, the most adept at politics, and the most comfortable in it. Both the order right and freedom left— the two positions suspicious of rationalist politics—turn away from politics to other spheres of activity as more important to both individual and social life: family, church, theater, art studio, coffeehouse. The dialectical sequence thus begins with a distaste for politics and government with the order right and ends in the same place with the freedom left.

In this chapter, I will explore the apparent contradictions within the left by recalling the decade of the 1960s, which began with the soaring, idealistic rhetoric of the order left and ended in the political and cultural anarchy of the freedom left. It will be important along the way to note how the governing idiom of that time moved quickly from the impersonal, political dreams of order liberals to the personal, cultural visions of freedom liberals.

The Decline of Authority

In 1960, when I was an undergraduate at Stanford, my classmates and I hadn't a care in the world. Ours was still a very traditional and innocent world, and it never occurred to us or most college students of that time to question its institutions and values. We did not go to college to question authority; we went to learn only what we needed to know about the world, so we could follow our fathers someday to become its leaders. The only forms of revolt one could find then were drinking parties and panty raids. Apathy was the first and only order of business. At the time, I must say, it seemed quite wonderful.

I first realized things were changing in the spring of 1961, the end of my junior year, when I ran for student body president. For the first time anyone could remember, candidates for student office (all of us) lamented the university's failures. We argued that the campus slumbered while important social problems remained unsolved; we had, to quote Robert Frost, "miles to go before we sleep." So we called people to action. We asked them to "get Stanford moving again!"

Jack Kennedy's dramatic accession to the White House had taken the campus by storm. The winning candidate for student body president, who tromped me in a runoff, modeled his campaign after JFK's—his rhetoric, his accent, everything.

The traditional order had begun to lose its legitimacy. It was losing its ability to inspire; its apolitical idealism could no longer motivate sacrifice.

During my senior year (1961–62), most of the members of Stanford's student leadership consciously identified with the order left vision of President Kennedy, regardless of our political backgrounds. We identified with him because he awakened us to a set of responsibilities very different from those of our parents' world. Protests against racial discrimination were mounting in the South, and we could see that the traditional ideal of "responsibility" had diverted our attention from a world rife with injustice. So, in my senior year, we spent much of our time seeking left-liberal causes to espouse: the problems of Cuba, South West Africa, Angola, the importance of the United Nations, a growing consciousness of race and poverty. We were fiercely idealistic, and our idealism was focused on and through politics, especially the politics of the federal government.

As traditional institutions and values began to lose their authority for students after 1960, the practice of student government, which had seemed so effortless before, all of a sudden became a big production. Rules proliferated; boards and councils were formed to perform judicial and appellate functions. As informal authority was collapsing, we relied more on rules and laws and formalized procedures to settle disputes that, in the past, had been settled casually.

Between 1960 and 1961, we students became "alienated." The quotation marks are necessary because, in the early 1960s, we were alienated only from the traditional order, which we wanted to change by using politics. At that time we felt no alienation from politics per se; on the contrary, our idealism sought entirely political outlets. In 1960 Stanford satisfied our need for belonging and community, and helped shape our identities. A year later—an incredibly short time later—it did not. The sense of positive community was gone, and the university administration had lost its authority. We went into open rebellion and built a new sense of community and belonging based on opposition to what we had known before.

It was the beginning of the 1960s as a political and social phenomenon, even though as the decade wore on this idealism changed very much. Later on, it would deteriorate into the ugliness and even hatred that at the end of the decade led many people to wonder whether America's democratic institutions would survive.

Looking back, the most conspicuous thing about the 1960s is that authority declined in all areas of life and in many different places at once. It happened in the United States and Europe and in many other parts of the world. It happened in politics but also in fashion, language, and even the standards of intellectual discourse and criticism. It was especially obvious in the arts—the plastic arts, music, movies, theater. It all seemed to begin abruptly in the middle of the decade, and most of it was over by the decade's end.

These changes also affected people individually and personally. The focus of many lives began to shift away from traditional responsibilities of job and family to the new responsibilities of political idealism. But as opposition to the traditional order grew, and as the decade wore on, the popular definition of the "traditional order" began to change. And after mid-decade, people looked less to politics and the order left as the principal instruments of their idealism, and more in other directions.

By 1964, cultural values were beginning to change subtly: fewer people were getting married, the birthrate began to decline, and the divorce rate was rising. Choices of work and life-style changed. In the 1950s, sons still followed their fathers into business, continuing a practice that had gone back centuries. In the 1960s, sons and (increasingly) daughters moved to different occupations, often different life-styles.

As people moved away from social responsibility toward personal expression, their opposition to traditional values, including the political idealism associated with the programs of the federal government, assumed increasingly extreme forms. In 1964, the year that followed President Kennedy's assassination, the Beatles and the miniskirt appeared. In December 1965 the first nudity was featured on Broadway (the Royal Shakespeare Theater production of *Marat Sade*), and movies began to portray more alienation and violence. Cultural protest followed political protest right through the end of the decade. The worst year of urban race riots (1967) and the first year of widespread student protests (1968) brought the most alienated films, the most extreme art, the most outrageous fashions. These changes were not limited to *avant-garde* cultural circles; in theater, for instance, they went straight to Broadway. In the spring of 1968 a musical featuring an entirely nude cast *(Hair)* played to sellout crowds. Sometimes theater directors went too far and public authorities balked, as they did when the entire cast and crew of the opening night Broadway performance of *Che!* was arrested for "obscenity, public lewdness, and consensual sodomy." But rarely.

Between 1964 and 1970 assaults on traditional values extended into every domain of social, moral, and aesthetic life. The authority of the family was challenged by women's liberation, legal abortion, institutionalized child care, and general demands for fundamental changes in the roles and responsibilities of men and women. Religious authority came under pressure when the Roman Catholic Church, that symbol of traditionalism, rewrote its liturgy and liberalized nearly all of its rules except those requiring celibacy for priests (which was widely ignored), and prohibiting artificial contraception for the laity (which was even more widely ignored).

A new emphasis on individual expression began to push ideas of social responsibility aside. The order left began to lose its authority soon after it gained power, and the left's energy shifted to its anti-political, freedom side. Although later admirers of President Kennedy denied he would have led us into the Vietnam War if he had lived, there is no doubt that it was precisely the idealism and sense of obligation of his order liberalism that got us into the war, and the anti-obligation tendency of freedom liberalism pushed hardest to get us out.

It is not surprising that these changes produced profound shifts in public attitudes, which were first reflected in public opinion polls around 1966. Through the end of the 1970s, polls showed a consistent decline of public confidence in all social institutions: government, medicine, business, education, science, labor, religion—everything.

But the new freedom impulse did not last long either. At the end of the 1960s, the freedom left lost its dominance as fast as it had risen to power. If hard or acid rock as played by the Rolling Stones and the Jefferson Airplane dominated music in 1968, by 1971 stars from the 1950s, such as Bill Haley and the Comets, Chuck Berry, and Chubby Checker, were making big comebacks. And *Hair* and *Che!* were replaced in the early 1970s by sentimental and nostalgic plays, and by the quasi-religious musicals *Jesus Christ Superstar* and *Godspell.* The theatrical sensation of 1971 was recycled from the 1920s— Busby Berkeley's *No, No, Nanette,* starring Ruby Keeler and several lavish production numbers. *Midnight Cowboy* and *Easy Rider* were the big movies of the end of the 1960s; in 1971 it was *Love Story,* a traditional tearjerker. At the same time women's fashions returned in nostalgia to the styles of a more traditional world: padded shoulders, platform shoes, veiled hats, and fur boas. By 1973, hemlines were down about where they were in 1962—around the knee. In *The Painted Word,* an exposé of the 1960s world of *avant-garde* art, Tom Wolfe told how artists and their patrons went crazy trying to stay *avant.*[1] But by the early 1970s, art, too, was calming down, and postmodernism was soon to follow.

Living in Amerika

During the 1960s, movements that now seem extreme were celebrated even in Establishment circles as expressions of the highest idealism.[2] While something much more complicated than simple idealism was involved, the tendency to *see* only idealism served as a reminder of how the old ideals of both the right and left had lost their power to inspire important segments of the population. This was especially evident toward the end of the decade, when major business and media figures celebrated youth and youth culture. The desperation that resulted from the loss of traditional meaning was perhaps most poignantly symbolized by the sight of aging swingers, sporting wild colors and huge mutton-chop sideburns.

The "generation gap" was big news, and its motto was "Never trust anyone over thirty." But the real gap had nothing to do with age; it was an attitude, a life-style, demonstrating opposition to traditional values of either the order left or the order right. In important respects, the media moved further and further away from the traditional order, especially in rejection of traditional sexual mores and the middle-class achievement ethic.

All of this involved an appeal to "freedom" and "honesty"—two of many buzzwords of the time, signifying liberation from traditional values—and these became the guiding aesthetic principles in fashion, film, theater, and music. Charles Reich's *The Greening of America* provided the period's chief philosophical statement, first serialized in the *New Yorker* magazine before being published as a book that sold more than a million copies. The most extreme expression of these new marginal values was represented at the end of the decade by deafening acid rock music and flashing strobe lights.

During the 1960s tensions rose in every sector of American society, and in most of the other Western democracies as well. Recriminations and blame were everywhere. Disagreements escalated into fanatical hatreds. By 1968, leaders of both major political parties wondered if America were not so fragmented as to be ungovernable. This sentiment followed from incredible conflict and division in the body politic, symbolized by frequent accusations, coming even from major public figures, that our government was committing genocide in Vietnam. Many challenged the legitimacy of our political and social system—going so far as to adopt the spelling "Amerika," to associate the United States with Nazi Germany.

As the decade wore on, the tension between the freedom and order wings of the left grew intolerable, and it soon became clear that the media were becoming the principal instruments in the freedom left's attacks on the traditional liberals in the administration. In this role the media were following their traditional role as challengers of those in power, regardless of ideology.

These media challenges were most obvious in their influence on the terms of the political debate. In the language they used, the media in effect endorsed all of the principal charges that the New Left leveled against the old. As a result, in the late 1960s our public understanding of every moral and political relationship was turned upside down. Legitimate authority was seen as illegitimate; victims of crime, when they were part of mainstream society, were portrayed as "aggressors"; violent change was called "idealistic." Almost nothing remained of legitimate authority, as opinion makers in the media and elsewhere commonly asserted that the violence of protesters and "the people" was legitimate, while the authority of the state to prevent it was illegitimate. The greatest problem in the country, Attorney General Ramsey Clark said at the time, was "police violence."

Black revolutionaries such as Angela Davis and George Jackson became cult heroes not despite their advocacy of violence, but because of it. Biased attitudes toward Davis or her revolutionary colleagues were never difficult to detect in the media, which regularly described black revolutionaries as "brilliant." Tom Wicker's description of Jackson as "a talented writer, a sensitive man, a potential leader, and a political thinker of great persuasiveness" stands as typical of the Establishment media's attitude toward the revolutionary left during that period. Representatives of the black middle class were never portrayed this way. The black middle class was invariably seen as lacking sensitivity and competence of any kind. They were untrue to themselves—"Uncle Toms."

A most straightforward assertion of the illegitimacy of the political system came, ironically, from someone who was sworn to serve that system—an associate justice of the United States Supreme Court, William O. Douglas: "We must realize that today's Establishment is the new George III. Whether it will continue to adhere to his tactics, we do not know. If it does, the redress, honored in tradition, is . . . revolution."[3] Justice Douglas further implicitly asserted the obligation to revolution by concluding one section of his book *Points of Rebellion* by comparing the "powers-that-be" to Hitler.

Even more extreme was Jean-Paul Sartre's famous apotheosis of violence as a challenge to the traditional order, in his celebrated preface to Frantz Fanon's *The Wretched of the Earth*. He embraced African violence directed against all Europeans, including himself, in the following terms:

> Make no mistake about it; by this fury, by this bitterness and spleen, by their ever-present desire to kill us, by the permanent tensing of powerful muscles which are afraid to relax *they have become men*. . . . Hatred, blind hatred, which is as yet an abstraction, is their only wealth. . . . This irrepressible violence . . . *is man recreating himself*.[4]

Such words seem today bizarre, they are so extreme. But many people did not think so when Sartre wrote them. They could only be understood against the backdrop of the divisions and conflict that tore families and friends apart, as civil society struggled to avoid terminal chaos.

The Struggle to Understand

In retrospect, it may seem hard to understand why certain ideas were treated with the seriousness they were. Because at precisely the moment when the turmoil reached its peak, it all evaporated in an instant. Life returned to something approaching normal: sex and violence were toned down in the theater and in films; realism returned to art; the miniskirt disappeared and hemlines returned to former levels; acid rock disappeared, the Fillmore Auditorium closed down, and the innocence of 1950s-style music came back.

What happened? Why did the violence and craziness end as abruptly as they had begun?

Conventional wisdom held that the 1960s ended because of cynicism and disillusionment. People (this line of argument claimed) simply gave up on "the system," which they concluded was unalterably corrupt. On its face, this view did not explain very much. After all, the New Left was a movement that, without money and without a machine, had forced an incumbent president to step aside, and turned our war policy completely around. What greater influence could one imagine?

Although many people struggled to explain what had happened, none of the explanations were very convincing, because none explained the generality of the trends—the pervasiveness of the deterioration. Neither did they explain the end of the turmoil and the return to normality. The 1960s generated a parade of presidential commissions analyzing each of the decade's problems as a discrete event, separate and isolated from all the others. Thus, their analyses identified causes that could not explain why many problems appeared to die down spontaneously, all at about the same time, at the end of the decade.

The Kerner Commission, for instance, concluded that white racism was responsible for the urban race riots, and that the only hope of preventing such violence in perpetuity was to enact a whole panoply of ambitious social programs. The commission's report was published in early 1968, following the worst summer of rioting. Yet although there were some disturbances after the assassination of Dr. Martin Luther King, Jr., by early summer of that year it was obvious the worst was over. Although the commission's conclusions may have been valuable for other reasons, they could not begin to explain why urban rioting suddenly subsided. (Few people, after all, seemed prepared to conclude that white racism had disappeared between 1967 and 1968.) Decades later, when some people tried to resurrect Kerner-like reasoning to explain the 1992 riots in Los Angeles, fears of spreading "rebellion" again proved exaggerated.

The anti-Establishment tone that suffused the arts in the 1960s was said to reflect more open, less repressive mores than those that had dominated the old order. Yet at the end of the decade, trends in film, theater, fashion, and art abandoned the new "openness" in favor of a revival of traditional forms.

The substantive analyses did not explain the ubiquity of the trends of the late 1960s, which cut across international boundaries and penetrated every domain of life. The patterns hint that the trends were somehow connected, that something systemic was happening. The abrupt end of protests, however, should have suggested that substantive problems were not the "cause."

What is most interesting is that, contrary to every Establishment prediction, political violence as a mass phenomenon largely ended with the election to the presidency of a man the Establishment (both the liberal media and moderate Republicans) had hated more than any other for more than twenty years: Richard Milhous Nixon. Although there were episodes of violent protest in the fall of 1969 and again around the time of the Kent State killings in the spring of 1970, such disturbances—and the highly politicized mood that accompanied them—began to die out with Nixon's election. Nixon: the man who epitomized the values that the Establishment left had argued were responsible for all of our policy crises, both in Vietnam and on race. Nixon: whose election liberal pundits had predicted would cause all hell to break loose.

Yet the apocalypse did not happen. For anyone who lived through the period, it quickly became clear that with Nixon's election the torment was somehow passing. Thereafter, political protest was mainly perpetrated by small bands of terrorists, such as the Weather Underground and the Black Panthers.

A special kind of "disillusionment" may indeed have played an important role in this. To understand this, it may be useful, for instance, to recall the intellectual left's extraordinary reaction to President Nixon's decision to visit China, announced in July 1971.

When the China trip was announced, intellectuals of the left expressed great unhappiness. On the one hand, the idea of the trip proposed by their archenemy Nixon represented a monumental capitulation to their generation-long arguments for normalized relations with China. On the other hand, however, Nixon was a symbol of all they detested, and they had severe difficulty accepting his conversion to the side of the angels. While journalists of the moderate left merely grumbled about the trip, the radical journal *Ramparts* addressed the trip's full symbolic meaning in a lead editorial entitled "Asian Tragedy." The editorial began:

> Suddenly the world situation has become harder to understand than anyone under 30 can remember. It didn't happen exactly overnight, but confusion definitely began to set in sometime last July, when President Nixon's advance man surfaced in Peking to

announce the impending goodwill appearance of the world's number one imperialist, in that capital of revolutionary purity.[5]

Ramparts identified a symbolic incongruity that not only made it impossible for the left to enjoy the event and revel in its own triumph, but actually tormented it and increased its loathing of Nixon. The left's reaction highlighted the fact that it had almost no interest in the substance of the meeting of Mao Zedong and Nixon. Its concern was that the two leaders had refused (incomprehensibly) to play their appointed moral roles. William Appleman Williams summarized liberal intellectuals' attitudes toward the would-be convert Nixon in an article in the *New York Review of Books* entitled "Just Who Is Nixon Anyway?" Writing just after the China trip, Williams agonized over the "reason for our unhappiness, anger and fear." "Being evil," he concluded, referring to the president, "is a heavy trip."[6]

It is hard to come to grips with the implications of these words because the *idea* of the China trip seems to have overwhelmed the *action*, with which it was in conflict. The trip violated the left's highest ideals, and it exposed the heart of what the left seeks: right actions; but even before that, right *spirit*. Nixon, ever since his days as a rabid (in the view of the left) anticommunist, and particularly since the "Checkers speech," had symbolized the narrow, parochial, mean-spirited side of the order right. Because he was still, in 1971, a symbol of these things, his decision to go to China mocked the symbolism of hope that the order left associated with China. And of course Mao, by agreeing to receive Nixon, violated the same spirit. For Mao's China, as *Ramparts* noted correctly, had been the very symbol of "revolutionary purity."

What spirit did Nixon and Mao defile? The spirit of revolutionary purity that for the left had seemingly integrated freedom and order, that apparently brought subjective and objective together. It was a *myth*, of course. We know now about the horrors of the Chinese Cultural Revolution, which was in full swing at that time. Yet in 1971 Mao's China was a symbolic promised land for many American intellectuals. That is, until Nixon went there: intellectuals of the left could never look at China the same way after Nixon profaned it.

What does the reaction to Nixon's China trip reveal about the role he may have played in bringing the 1960s to an end? In trying to understand how the man universally reviled on the left managed to oversee the end of the nightmare, we might do well to view the America of the time as suffering from a manic-depressive disorder. The 1960s began with mania, in which the whole of American society went on a high. In this period the expectations of both the freedom and order left pushed everyone toward wanting "more": more social legislation, more troops in Vietnam, more colorful clothing, longer hair, louder music, more sex.

President Nixon's election seemed to bring all this to an end by injecting a severe depressant into the exhilarations of the period. As a symbol of the "reactionary" culture, he could do certain things— de-escalate the Vietnam War, approach China—that yielded to liberal desires. He could get away with these things because, unlike the gestures of more liberal presidents, Nixon's actions did not fuel the left's manic passions. The *idea* of Nixon as a symbol of the old, repressed, internalized culture was enough to introduce a new sense of stability and order into a society that had been out of control. Nixon seemed to confound the chaos of the political and moral system of the late 1960s. His trip to China confused the intellectual left utterly, diffused its anger, and (it would seem) encouraged much of it to withdraw from politics altogether. The nation calmed; the long, dark night of the 1960s could finally end.

This tension between the substance of Nixon's program, which continued on in the same general (liberal) direction as that of his predecessors, and the myth of his program (that is, the left's perception of it) was exhibited in the highest possible relief in early 1972 in two *New York Times* editorials, published only six weeks apart— one speaking to the substantive issue and the other to the symbolic. On January 31, 1972, an editorial crowed over the president's relinquishment of the substance of every conservative position he had ever held, and his simultaneous embrace of every position of the Democratic left: "In its abandonment of outmoded conservative doctrine," the editors intoned, "the Nixon administration has moved much more swiftly and thoroughly than did the Eisenhower administration." Nevertheless, when an occasion arose on March 22 to reaffirm Nixon's symbolic role as archconservative, an editorial made the following comment on Representative Ogden Reid's decision to leave the Republican party and become a Democrat: "That Mr. Reid has decided he can no longer stay in the [Republican] Party," the editors wrote, "is graphic evidence of how far to the right it has drifted under the leadership of President Nixon."

The Beginnings of the Decline

When the New Left first surfaced, its opposition to the order left did not take the form of direct criticism of Washington, even though its ideals were very different from those that animated Washington policy makers. The first civil disobedience was in protest only of university policies. Nevertheless, by the time of the emergence of the Berkeley Free Speech Movement in the fall of 1964, the signs were already clear that something much larger was afoot.

Ostensibly concerned with assuring the right to recruit volunteers for political movements on campus, the Free Speech Movement in fact sprang from rising dissatisfaction with and alienation from society as a whole. It flowed directly from the trends I began to see at Stanford in the spring of 1961. FSM leader Mario Savio expressed the broader problem in relation to the civil rights movement in the following terms:

> What oppresses the American Negro community is merely an exaggerated, grotesque version of what oppresses the rest of the country—and this is eminently true of the middle class, despite its affluence. The Berkeley students now demand what hopefully the rest of an oppressed white middle class will some day demand: freedom for all Americans, not just for Negroes![7]

A number of surveys of FSM activists revealed that much more concerned them than the narrow issue of the right to engage in political activity on a particular sidewalk. Asked if dissatisfaction with the university was really the problem, even most FSM activists suggested otherwise, and expressed considerable satisfaction with the education they were getting.[8]

The freedom left reacted to the Establishment left's preoccupation with rationalism and mechanistic policy, which were the governing allegiances of the Kennedy-Johnson administrations. It did not react to the failures of the order left in power, however. In fact, as I have noted, the New Left began its reaction early in the Kennedy-Johnson period—in 1962, long before any major policy initiatives had been enacted, and therefore long before there were any signs that they would fail. Rather, the reaction came as part of the left's (and the rest of society's) larger, ongoing search to integrate freedom and order. It was part of a search for a way to encourage people freely and individually to embrace a vision of the higher good, one that included all of the great socialist (and traditional religious) ideals.

Such a vision requires development of self-governing individuals and groups, however; it cannot be realized by any mechanistic, "Newtonian" initiative to fix the great policy-making machine in Washington, D.C. Public and political action can implement change only in the realm of the external and the objective; it cannot enjoin individuals to embrace internal and subjective changes. Yet such changes of *spirit* are precisely what the realization of a new, integrated vision requires.

That the liberal government of President Kennedy began with a program focused on achieving order simply reflected the left's "superior function." But the intensity with which the administration labored for order guaranteed that it would not be long before the freedom liberals would react.

The New Left's movement away from politics was a dialectical reaction to the Establishment left's grand vision of an ideal society built from the top down, relying almost entirely on the federal government as its mechanism. This vision incorporated all of the ideas that had been dominant in progressive thinking since the Enlightenment: reason, individualism, science, centralization, mechanistic policy, material progress, and the right of man to dominate nature. The new freedom left rejected all of these ideas.

Although many observers of the conflict between the old left and the new saw the two as separate phenomena, what I discern are complementary tendencies of the left. But the 1960s showed how, in their search for reconciliation, the freedom left and order left can be driven to extreme conflict whenever either comes to power. As I have already noted, the same is true of the right: when either the freedom or order right gains power, the other feels excluded and rebels.

This conflict is inevitable because serious reconciliation of these positions is impossible through centralized politics; reconciliation can only take place outside of it. The reason for this is that in any integration one can imagine of freedom and order, individuals and smaller, intermediate institutions must play the dominant roles. Central governments can and should establish the underlying rules of a productive order. They can also provide basic social protections. But they cannot be the guiding force in promoting positive experiences of community, as they so often try to be today.

The Left's Current Dilemma

The dilemma of the left in the United States is the dilemma of the order left. In a country that is inherently liberal (in the classical sense), the order left can thrive only given an economic catastrophe such as the Great Depression. Without an open social upheaval, it has a great problem selling its centralizing policies to a populace that has always distrusted powerful central governments. The order left's dilemma comes from its reflexive desire to throw money at problems. This instinct is in complete contrast to liberal society's focus on self-governing individuals and communities.

This perspective suggests that the future of the left lies with the descendants of the New Left, which sought during the 1960s to build self-governing institutions among minority groups, the disadvantaged, and even the middle class. It may lie, in fact, in exactly the same place as the future of the right. For as I pointed out at the end of the previous chapter, growing numbers of libertarian conservatives are working to accomplish very similar objectives. Moreover, the most imaginative of them—people such as Hernando de Soto in Peru and Leon Louw in South Africa, Robert Woodson in Washington, D.C., and Robert B. Hawkins, Jr., in San Francisco—have almost separated themselves from the mainstream of the right. Without abandoning their conservative principles, they are today focusing their energies on working in partnership with the left.

A striking example of emerging leftist interest in self-governance appeared when *Telos,* for decades America's preeminent non-Leninist Marxist journal, devoted its entire spring 1992 issue to exploring federalism as a solution to our political crisis. *Telos* editor Paul Piccone has in fact personally spearheaded this rising interest in decentralization and self-governance.

An alliance between descendants of the New Left and the new conservative idealists is in its infancy; but its inherent logic explains its success. Given the need to work through individuals and small groups to integrate freedom and order, this alliance should grow and become increasingly powerful.

As this new coalition is gaining strength, the left remains torn by contradictions that have recently seemed more incapacitating than those within the right. The left continues to experience electoral difficulties when it invests more of its identity in now unpopular, centralized politics than does the right. This explains the superficial impression that all Western societies are becoming more conservative.

Deeper trends, however, are pushing society in the other direction, toward the left. Environmentalism and feminism are two movements that have powerful and growing constituencies. The constellation of issues loosely defined as multiculturalism, including the new concern for the rights of groups rather than individuals, continues to exercise strong influence on the political debate—again reflecting the influence of the left.

But more important than these topical concerns is the failure of the so-called turn to the right to touch intellectuals or those who identify with them, who voted in overwhelming numbers against both President Reagan and President Bush. These people continue to hearken to ideals of the left. They are growing, and will continue to grow, in strength.

Intellectuals remain inspired by my generation's demand for individual freedom. Freedom, however, requires assumption of the burden of choice. Freedom is exhilarating, even intoxicating; but it brings its own troubles. It forces people to confront—every day, sometimes even when they are not aware of it—the deepest questions of life. It also breeds dissaffection from established moral authority. Although the decline of traditional authority and values is occurring in societies everywhere, it has reached a point of crisis in the West. This is because the Judeo-Christian religious tradition and the middle-class achievement ethic have lost their hold not only on major segments of the opinion-making elite, but also on an increasing portion of the general public. All economic and social trends suggest that the decline will continue, if not accelerate.

These trends result from the logic of economic growth, which depends on continuing investments in what economists call "human capital." Economic growth is transforming industrial societies into postindustrial, information economies, which will be run at all levels by "knowledge workers": people who resemble alienated intellectuals in education, life-style, and basic values. It is ironic that economic growth, which conservatives by and large support, should be a major cause of increasingly widespread hostility to the traditional institutions and values that conservatives cherish. But that is the reality.

The ultimate question is: Can new sources of authority and order be found without resort to the authoritarian and even totalitarian ideologies that have so afflicted this century? That question haunts modern society. If we cannot answer it, the crisis of social authority in the 1960s will have provided only a taste of what we will face again in the future.

Although the worst of the 1960s is behind us, we still live with its legacy. The weakness of the old Establishment became obvious during that decade, when important public figures made it clear they felt uncomfortable in their roles and wanted to join the radical opposition. We have pulled back from those days, but signs are everywhere of continued weakness in the traditional order. If new forms of authority and values are not found—new forms that are consistent with individual freedom and encourage it—then it will be only a matter of time before people will demand that authority and order be imposed on them. This is what happened at the end of the 1960s, and the tendency toward it is what underlies the notions of "political correctness" found on university campuses today. Some observers may believe that the end of history is at hand, that liberal democracy has won, and that there is nowhere else for society to go. Unfortunately, however, the continuing decline of traditional forms of order is pushing many people to redefine liberal democracy, and their redefinitions bear little resemblance to that ideal as we have known it for most of our lives.

4

Order without Collectivism

In trying to understand the modern crisis of values, both the order left and the order right—the social democratic left and the traditional right, which are both often suspicious of capitalism—puzzle about what has "gone wrong" in human society. Although they begin with very different judgments about the nature of man, they come to surprisingly similar conclusions about the solution to his problems.

To simplify greatly, the left, after Rousseau, believes man is born free and good, but is corrupted by institutions—meaning traditional institutions. Conservatives, on the other hand, take original sin as their starting point: they believe that man is born flawed and needs institutions and tradition to contain his appetites. Despite this difference in judging what has gone wrong, the order wings of both left and right come to interestingly similar conclusions: both blame misdirected freedom and individualism for encouraging preoccupation with self and disregard for higher values. And both, therefore, opt for collectivism as the solution—collective solutions imposed on individuals. The order left does this in its reliance on the central state, and the order right does it by urging a return to traditional institutions, especially traditional religion.

It is important to be clear that only the order left and order right are preoccupied by the crisis of values. The freedom wings worry about it, but indirectly and in a different way. Both freedom left and freedom right see collectivism as a problem, not the solution.

The difficulty this split causes within both the left and the right may easily be imagined. In a letter to a friend, the converted Catholic and former communist Whittaker Chambers once affirmed that he was a "man of the right," not a "conservative," because, he said, he could never support capitalism.[1] His distinction reflects modern conservatism's hybrid nature, a union of classical liberals (freedom conservatives) and traditional conservatives (order conservatives). Although often concealed in public debate, his view is commonly held by order conservatives. In this respect, order conservatives sound more like socialists than like freedom conservatives, whose commitment is to the free market.

A similar split characterizes the modern left. Although the United States has never had a strong socialist tradition, American intellectuals have nevertheless been influenced in important ways by socialist ideas—they have looked to socialist thought to offer the moral authority and communal obligation formerly provided by traditional authority, especially religion. In one of his last books, the late Michael Harrington recalled Marx's own belief that socialism could serve as a secular substitute for religion; and countless observers of Marxism have noted its "religious" appeal, especially its appeal to spiritual longing.

Although intellectuals drew on socialism to provide society with new purpose and meaning, they sought to do more than simply reestablish order. To make an advance over traditional forms of order, it was felt, socialism had to bring individual freedom as well. The path to freedom, however, was seen to require creation of new economic and social institutions that overthrew the stifling economic and moral system associated with bourgeois capitalism. Socialism was thus, above all, the weapon of those who saw in capitalism the source of all the modern world's troubles.

Capitalism's socialist and nonsocialist critics argue that "the profit system" destroys what we now call the "quality of life." The old left decries the destruction of relationships among people, arguing that capitalism makes them more self-centered, more materialistic, less interested in higher values. Criticism of capitalism for despoiling the environment is a variation on this theme.

The trouble with this view is that such alienation is as evident (perhaps more so) in socialist countries as in capitalist countries. And, as a result, the crisis of values is also just as common (perhaps more so) in socialist countries. It is also less evident in premodern, preindividualist societies than in modern, individualist ones—it is more evident in the United States and Russia than in Indonesia or Burma; more evident in socialist Cuba and Vietnam than in capitalist Singapore and Taiwan.

A closer look at these issues will reveal that today's crisis of values has nothing whatever to do with "capitalist" or "socialist" institutions. It is a by-product of individualism, and arises to the extent that a people is modern and not traditional. Moreover, this crisis is most sharply felt among intellectuals and artists, not among those who continue in large measure to live by tradition and habit.

Solving this and other problems that result from modern individualism requires understanding their source. Most important, we must stop blaming fictitious enemies; we must stop blaming "systems." The real source of these problems is in us, as we search for a way to integrate the modern emphasis on individual self-expression with a vision of values, community, and purpose that transcends the individual self—a way to integrate freedom and order.

Capitalism and socialism have a role to play in the search for a solution. I will argue that capitalism and socialism represent not conflicting, but complementary, ideas. The real conflicts are, in fact, *within* each idea—between the freedom element and the order element in each—which push against each other as they struggle for reconciliation, even as the same conflicts do so within the left and the right.

To understand these relationships, we would do well to recall the historical context in which capitalism and socialism began to conflict.

The Historical Background

The origins of modern socialism may be found in the Renaissance, when man was turning away from faith and toward reason. This was long before there was any "left" hostile to capitalism. From its initial stirrings in the fourteenth century, capitalism and the emerging middle class it fostered were seen to embody only freedom, at odds with the traditional order. Modern socialist opposition to capitalism began only at the end of the eighteenth century, when capitalism had become the principal instrument of the Industrial Revolution. When it was seen as bringing freedom, capitalism was considered redemptive; but when it became identified with industrialization, a concept of order, capitalism became for socialists the cause of all that was wrong with the modern world.

To understand why many intellectuals turned against capitalism at that time, it is important to recall the attractions of the life that ended with industrialization.

Preindustrial life featured a social order built on the authority of family and church, which were as secure as social life was stable. Modern life is torn by questions of purpose and meaning, but traditional life was protected from these by religion and religious values. In *The Communist Manifesto,* Marx and Engels lamented the loss of this stability and blamed capitalism:

> The bourgeoisie . . . has pitilessly torn asunder the motley feudal ties that bound man to his "natural superiors," and has left remaining no other nexus between man and man than naked self-interest, than callous "cash payment." It has drowned the most heavenly ecstasies of religious fervor, of chivalrous enthusiasm, of philistine sentimentalism, in the icy water of egotistical calculation.[2]

Marx, like all socialists, argued that capitalism is to blame for egotism and materialism, inflaming concern for one's own good and destroying the longing for the higher values of the common good.

This admiration of traditional societies was echoed during the 1960s, when anthropologists such as Margaret Mead encouraged people to look to them for clues as to how modern industrial societies could solve their problems. A virtual parade of people expressed this sentiment and longing when they traveled from Europe and the United States to China during the Cultural Revolution and returned with rhapsodic tales about brotherhood and community and, as James Reston put it, efforts to "bring out the best in man, what makes him good."[3]

Even many defenders of capitalism agree that capitalism either is inherently materialistic or at least that it encourages materialism.

Joseph Schumpeter, a champion of capitalism, provided one of the most sophisticated statements of this position when he predicted capitalism would eventually die because its relentless rationalization of relations between people made "emotional attachment" to it impossible.[4] When businessmen defensively assert that "profit" is not a "dirty word," they nevertheless implicitly concede that capitalism is inherently materialistic. It is no wonder that Daddy Warbucks and Ebenezer Scrooge remain archetypal capitalist symbols.

But are materialism and greed distinctive to capitalism? Does socialism protect people from greed? Of course not. On the contrary, socialism hands all property rights to people who become (in fact, if not in name) monopoly capitalists. This explains much of the crisis of socialism in the Eastern bloc countries: the *nomenklatura* (governing class) in those countries shamelessly enjoyed their limousines, their *dachas,* and their access to foreign exchange and special medicine, while ordinary people lived like serfs. Why should anyone have been surprised several years ago when Daniel Ortega, president of the revolutionary Sandinista government in Nicaragua, came to New York and purchased $2,500 worth of revolutionary eyewear?

There is a more fundamental reason why socialism offers no protection from materialism and greed. It is because the "order" socialism that supposedly offers this protection represents only part of the socialist vision. There is another side—the "freedom" side— that is also part of socialism, an indispensable part. The freedom side of socialism offers no such protection, because it can offer none. Protection against materialism ultimately depends on an integration of nonmaterialistic values with freedom. Socialists have never successfully accomplished the reconciliation.

Freedom Socialism and Order Socialism

Part of the socialist tradition emphasizes the objective, the material, the rational, the scientific—things of the mind. Another part of the tradition stresses the subjective, the spontaneous, the expressive, the emotional—things of the spirit. The first of these tendencies is concerned with order, the second with freedom. The first finds its most extreme expression in the "scientific socialism" of the former Eastern bloc countries; the second finds it in the counterculture socialism that was especially evident in the West during the 1960s.

Freedom socialists are easy to identify. They are descendants of the New Left of the 1960s—suspicious of "bigness" in all its forms (both in the government and in business), alienated from the mainstream of society, pursuing highly individual life-styles. They are anarchists and the counterculture, concentrating in their own sections of major cities or retreating to the countryside. They are antipolitical, and this, perhaps more than anything else, sets them apart from order socialists, whom they detest as much as they detest the captains of industry.

Pure order socialists are hard to find in the 1990s in the United States; they were far more common in the 1930s and 1940s. Nevertheless, the liberal wing of the Democratic party has been greatly influenced by the order socialists of an earlier era. Order socialists still look to central governments to restore values and reduce inequalities they believe are caused by capitalism. Even in 1992, despite his extraordinary efforts as the Democratic presidential nominee to distance himself from the order left, Bill Clinton often attacked his Republican opponent for aggravating inequality; and the centerpiece of Clinton's economic program called for spending several hundred billion dollars of federal money for what he called "investment" in physical and human "infrastructure."

The problem is that such collectivism is no longer believed to work, even by socialists. Socialists have come to know, finally, that imposed order, without free choice, cannot satisfy modern people. Modern people need a new form of order, consistent with freedom.

Order socialists today avoid advocating the dreary, centralized utopias that were once popular with them. They talk abstractly about decentralization, not saying how they would accomplish it, while focusing their concrete proposals on centralized action to realize their dreams of equality and brotherhood.

Centralized, Leninist state socialism is as far removed from the counterculture as the counterculture is from the capitalism of the Gilded Age. Both extremes of socialism are, in fact, nightmares. Socialism without freedom offers only the dystopias of *1984* and *Brave New World*. Socialism without a vision of order—of community, equality, and brotherhood—can yield only hyper-individualistic nihilism. Socialism's future appeal thus depends on reconciling and integrating these very different visions.

What do the two sides of socialism have in common? Both are modern and egalitarian, opposed to the hierarchical basis of traditional society. In different ways, both offer a vision of community that provides a sense of purpose and good that is intended to bind together individuals alienated from tradition. But without the integration of its freedom and order tendencies, socialism has usually been identified only in its order form, for order is the superior function of the left.

Even though it can achieve nothing positive without the integration of its two tendencies, order socialism has powerful meaning for its adherents in its opposition to capitalism, which all socialists blame for modern alienation. But if socialism means only the negation of capitalism, it cannot avoid ideological incoherence unless its opposite, capitalism, means something coherent. Unfortunately, it does not—for capitalism likewise remains split into freedom and order tendencies.

Freedom Capitalism and Order Capitalism

The word "capitalism" conjures up strong images of wealth: Wall Street, big business, John D. Rockefeller. Wealth is associated with capitalism not only because we commonly think of capitalists as wealthy, but also because capitalism has made Europe, the United States, and now growing numbers of Asian countries rich. This fact explains why most of the world's remaining "communist" countries are becoming increasingly capitalist in their search for prosperity.

But while images of great wealth are strongly associated with capitalism, they miss an important part—an essential part—of capitalism as it is defined by economists. Let me present the point in the form of a question: How should we understand the role of small-scale enterprises in preindustrial times and today? Are they "capitalist"? The images of wealth just mentioned apply only to the giants of industrial capitalism. Where does the mom-and-pop grocery store fit in? The enormous and obvious differences between the two types of enterprise suggest it may be more confusing than clarifying to categorize them both as "capitalist."

Small and large private enterprises have in common that both are owned by independent citizens, not the government. While this is an important commonality, it may be more important in theory than in practice. In important respects, we use the word "capitalist" to mean two completely different things—just as we do with the word "socialist."

What bonds small and large enterprises is dependence on the market: this represents the heart of an economist's understanding of capitalism. The power of the market is very great, and one can appreciate it by observing its effects on both large and small enterprises. There are two grocery stores in my neighborhood. One is owned by a huge conglomerate; the other is a nonprofit cooperative. Which store would you guess has lower prices? The answer is that their prices are the same. The reason for this is that if one or the other charged consistently lower prices for the same service (including ambiance), it would get all the business; and the other would go under. The market is an instrument of freedom, because people can use it to choose the value of anything they want. The market represents the freedom sense of capitalism.

There is another understanding of capitalism that is held particularly by businesspeople, and this refers to the institutions and values commonly associated with corporate capitalism. The relationship between these different concepts of capitalism may be easiest to understand in relation to their socialist counterparts:

	Freedom	Order
Capitalism	free markets	large corporations
Socialism	street vendors	central government

The two conceptions of capitalism—freedom capitalism and order capitalism—could hardly be more different.

People associated with order capitalism identify with traditional values—the middle-class achievement ethic and traditional (frequently religious) values. In the contemporary American political spectrum, commitment to order capitalism is thus a central component of traditional conservatism. The counterculture, which is alienated from traditional values, is the extreme example of a group opposed by order capitalists.

Freedom capitalism, in contrast, deals not in corporate institutions and values, but in the freedom to choose whatever one values, material or nonmaterial, traditional or nontraditional. Freedom capitalism, which is embraced by libertarian conservatives, thus counts the counterculture as capitalist, while rejecting many practices of big business as anticapitalist.

Counterculturalists are quintessential freedom capitalists because they regularly participate, far removed from the world of government favors, in one of the purest forms of market capitalism left in the world: the extensive markets that have developed in handcrafted artifacts, organic food products, specialized clothing, day-care services, and other things counterculturalists value. These markets bring tears of admiration to the eyes of market economists, since their freedom of exchange is rarely found in larger enterprises.

On the other hand, many corporate businessmen are ambivalent if not actually hostile to capitalism, or at least capitalism in its free dom sense. Although most businessmen praise the free market and condemn government interference in it, in their own particular cases (that is, when government interference would aid them) they can usually find special circumstances that make intervention a matter of overriding public interest. Trucking industry executives, for example, are prominent among those denouncing government intervention in the economy; yet no subject angers them more than proposals for the deregulation of trucking. They are order, not freedom, capitalists.

Again, without integration of its freedom and order tendencies, "capitalism" is a word without coherent meaning. Yet it is clear from the rate at which large corporations are losing their markets to small, entrepreneurial companies that capitalism's freedom side is dominant—as is the case with the political right.

Idealism and Materialism

In the contemporary political debate, many intellectuals are attracted to socialist idealism and decry capitalist realism as representing a mass culture obsessed by materialism and status seeking. They see the archetypal member of the middle class as the Man in the Grey Flannel Suit, the Organization Man; as "other-directed," driven by a need to "keep up with the Joneses." Most important, they attack the middle class for its indifference to higher values.

In an important sense, this view distorts the reality of most traditional middle-class people; such ambitious individualism more appropriately characterizes intellectuals themselves. Middle-class values, at least in their (undebased) traditional form, come with a strong dose of Puritanism, which attached importance to frugality and modest living. The middle-class achievement ethic is largely a standard of personal virtue, based not on comparisons with others, but on commitment to absolute moral values ratified (originally) by religious convictions. This ethic is, for instance, the distinguishing characteristic of the heroes in Horatio Alger's novels.

The middle class has nothing like the achievement ambitions of most intellectuals. The middle class has God and family—even though these allegiances are imperfect and (for many) becoming weaker. In particular, the middle class is blessed with a relatively unquestioning acceptance of traditional values—matter-of-fact notions of right and wrong—because it has a largely objective view of the world and of reality, and because it is relatively undisturbed by a subjective drive to question and understand. Middle-class people want mainly to "make good" and live "a good life." Thus, materialism, in the sense of the longing for external rewards, is not all that important to the middle class.

On the other hand, intellectuals' resentment of the achievement ethic arises precisely because ambition is the only value many intellectuals have. Because they are driven by a need to validate reality subjectively, and are thus torn by skepticism, intellectuals often lack the higher values, especially religious values, that the middle class gets from tradition. As a result, many intellectuals define themselves individually through external achievement, through self-assertion.

Underlying the difference between these two groups is the inability of intellectuals to live according to tradition and their need to make conscious choices about moral and social life. Traditional economic and religious life is driven largely by habit, and it is for that reason alienating to most intellectuals.

In fact, two different kinds of morality are evident here: the traditional morality of nonintellectual people and the political morality of most intellectuals. The differences between them are both substantive (relating to essence) and instrumental (relating to practice). Substantively, traditional morality concerns one's relations to one's kin by blood or belief—family, tribe, and church—while modern political morality emphasizes relations that reach across ethnic and religious boundaries—even, in some cases, to encompass the whole world. Substantively, the size and proximity of the community to which moral obligations are due are very different.

Instrumentally, traditional morality exhorts one to fulfill one's own responsibilities to others, while political morality looks to political institutions to accomplish economic and social good. There are difficulties with both ethics. Traditional morality often excludes obligations to "outsiders," while political morality often allows its adherents to preach values that they do not themselves practice (as when the same person who acclaims world peace mistreats his maid).

In this discussion I have considered the middle class as an ideal. The middle class possessed of its own traditional morality is almost certainly disappearing, especially in urban areas. The reason for this is that the postindustrial middle class—especially in its contemporary "yuppie" incarnation—is taking on psychosocial characteristics increasingly like those of intellectuals.

Since intellectuals are engaged in a constant search for an idealism to which they can ascribe, they actually feel hostility to only one of capitalism's faces: to order capitalism, with its attachment to bourgeois values and to "realism." Neoconservatives are among the few intellectuals who defend what I call order capitalism, but even they do so without much enthusiasm. (Neoconservative godfather Irving Kristol gives it only "two cheers," not three.)[5]

On the other hand, many intellectuals are enthusiastic in their embrace of freedom capitalism. The idealistic possibilities in freedom capitalism are great—as suggested by Milton Friedman's celebration of the Israeli kibbutz ideal as a triumph of capitalism. He does so because the kibbutz is based on free choice, the central commitment of freedom capitalism.

What are commonly referred to as "capitalist values" and "socialist values" make sense only in relation to the order concepts of capitalism and socialism. They make no sense at all in relation to the freedom versions. Even the left's hostility to profit is limited to profit's association with order capitalism. Only the most fanatical socialist objects to the profit earned by selling handmade clothing or health food, because traffic in these products is not supportive of an order inimical to socialism.

It is important to note here that freedom capitalists (for example, street vendors) don't have "capitalist values" either. In fact, the longer you look at them, the more difficult it is to differentiate between freedom capitalists and freedom socialists.

Although socialists attack profit as debasing relations between people, in the economist's sense profits do precisely the opposite. Profit facilitates cooperation, serving as a signaling mechanism that enables buyers to tell sellers quickly and forcefully what they want. The willingness to supply profit is what gives buyers leverage over sellers and ensures that there is real cooperation. When either party professes itself to be "above" such commercial motivations, the result can often be a disastrous failure in cooperation.

The following story will make the essential lesson here more concrete.

The Zen Carpenter

I once knew a young carpenter who was strongly influenced by the counterculture's hostility to capitalism, which he believed encouraged materialism and greed, and made higher values impossible to attain. Moreover, his hostility to the commercial world was not merely abstract. He had a singular contempt for others in his trade, whom he accused of not sharing his Zen-inspired devotion to quality and of charging too much for their services. He, in contrast, was committed to living his ideal, determined to avoid the self-seeking he saw all around him.

I met the carpenter, whom I shall call Jack, when he began some remodeling work for a friend of mine (Susan), who shared the young carpenter's ideals completely. They shared E. F. Schumacher's *(Small Is Beautiful)* vision, and their shared ideals greatly increased the enthusiasm with which they undertook the remodeling project. In it, both were determined to avoid the behaviors they associated with capitalism.

From the beginning Jack was true to his creed. He thus began by bidding the job fairly—he underbid it, that is, anticipating that he would simply absorb a number of costs that he did not include in his estimates. Susan was pleased with the bid, and Jack began work.

Problems appeared when it became obvious Jack would not finish in the time agreed. In his desire to please and to live by his ideals, his commitment to quality was leading him to choose far more expensive materials and building techniques than either he or my friend could afford.

Costs rose. Jack ran out of money and asked Susan to advance him more—emphasizing to her the high quality of workmanship she was receiving. The work went on. Susan moved out of her apartment and began living with friends. Jack promised the work would be done the first week of November. Then the third week. Estimates of time and money escalated. He encountered new problems.

At the end of January, Susan was in trauma. Jack continued to insist that the job was only hours short of completion, but it somehow never got completed. Finally, in desperation, Susan hired another carpenter—a hard-nosed, no-nonsense type, who came in and finished the work in two weeks, with Jack working alongside him.

What had gone wrong? Many things, of course—not all Jack's fault, not all foreseeable. The essential problem, however, was Jack's failure to understand that his commitment to "quality" had nothing to do with the "quality" Susan wanted—which was strongly influenced by what she could afford. While Jack's commitment might be seen as idealistic, it was in fact entirely selfish, because he made no real effort to help Susan—to cooperate with her—to do what she wanted. During the job, relations between them deteriorated to the point where they were not speaking.

Traditional views of capitalism and socialism explain nothing about what happened between these two people. One way of looking at their experience is as a conflict between his idealism and her desire for cooperation. But the longer we think about the situation, the harder it is to see Jack's desire to impose his values on Susan as representing any idealism.

Capitalism and Socialism as Complementary

If neither capitalism nor socialism is coherent without (at least) some integration of its freedom and its order tendencies, it becomes easy to see why (failing that integration) each has effective meaning only as a negation of the other.

The conclusion that capitalism and socialism have meaning only as negations of their opposites leads into a circular dilemma in which it becomes hard to find any meaning at all. Yet the struggle over issues of freedom and order both within and between capitalism and socialism highlights the essential need for integration. In the end, it becomes clear that capitalism and socialism represent not conflicting, but complementary ideologies—capitalism, with freedom as its superior function, socialism tending toward order—struggling for reconciliation with each other. They struggle for the same integration as do the political right and left.

That capitalism and socialism are complementary conflicts with all standard understandings of these ideologies. But seeing them this way clarifies many puzzles that otherwise remain unsolved. Recall that Schumpeter argued that capitalism, because of the market's value-neutrality, lacks any means of encouraging emotional attachment to itself. Why, then, are people everywhere turning away from socialism? The reason is that socialism, without integration of its freedom and order sides, cannot command emotional allegiance either.

Emotional allegiance to an idea depends on its vision—the sense it conveys of striving for something better. Such idealism requires both a substantive vision of the good (which the market lacks) and an instrumental commitment to freedom (which traditional socialism lacks). Virtue or order without freedom implies authoritarianism. Freedom without virtue or order means nihilism and license. Each value is incomplete without the other. Since order is primarily represented by socialism and freedom chiefly by capitalism, it becomes clear that socialism and capitalism are important not for the conflict between them, but for their part in an unfolding, dialectical search for resolution. Only when these two ideologies are combined can a meaningful, complete idealism be found—only then will there be a possibility of emotional allegiance to either.

Some might say that such a libertarian socialism would require a hopelessly idealistic belief in the human capacity to choose the good. But the belief of traditional socialists that truly public-spirited, selfless bureaucrats can be found to administer a genuinely socialist state seems no less idealistic. The difference is that in a decentralized system any lack of public spirit has only local consequences; in a centralized system, a brutalizing ripple effect touches everyone and everything. The latter point is made clear by the struggle of the former Eastern bloc countries to cast off order socialism.

It is true that few of capitalism's defenders stress the idealism I have considered here. This is a major weakness. Those who care about capitalism should work overtime to reinvest it with a vision of virtue and a commitment to the good life. Proponents who would bind capitalism to man's lowest instincts and aspirations— and even celebrate the vulgarization of freedom, as Ayn Rand did inconsistently—only encourage the myth that capitalism is intrinsically materialistic. Such supporters thereby collaborate in slandering capitalism.

Understanding the modern impossibility of collectivizing

virtue—and perceiving the challenge of achieving order without collectivism—is essential to understanding why traditional (order) socialism and (order) capitalism so often deteriorate into authoritarianism. If one understands that the crises of politics and of values come as a result of the advance of individualism—which brings a corresponding increase in the need of people to make free, subjective choices about social and moral life—then one will see that solutions lie beyond the collectivism proposed by the socialist left and the traditionalist right.

5

The Crisis of the Centralized State

Breakdown and crisis are rife in our politics. Signs of this are everywhere. They may be seen in the triviality of current political discourse; the disappearance of meaningful electoral choice (in recent times, more than 95 percent of congressional representatives seeking reelection have won it every two years, and one of every five has run unopposed); the collapse (until the East-West conflict ended) of a bipartisan American foreign policy; the incapacity of Congress to agree on annual budgets and its chronic reliance on continuing resolutions; and the increasing abdication by Congress of decision-making responsibilities (which it leaves to the courts). Perhaps the most dramatic recent sign of the breakdown of our national government was the violation of trust between the executive and legislative branches over Irangate, which echoed the Watergate scandal and cover-up of the early 1970s.

The breakdown of our politics is in fact the outward manifestation of the crisis of the centralized state. To understand this, it is important to recall how much our politics is affected by our preoccupation with the federal government and our relative indifference to all other levels and dimensions of governance. Thus the recent presidential campaigns had almost nothing to say about governance at the local level; the candidates of both parties emphasized the primacy of federal rules, laws, and institutions. They were almost entirely unconcerned with the myriad ways in which federal laws unnecessarily preempt and reduce state and local authority. This was true both for President Bush, who called, in the main, for reducing the size of government, and Governor Clinton, who called for increasing it.

Our fixation on the federal government also explains why our political system, like an investigative reporter, is preoccupied with exposing falsehood and has almost no interest in exploring positive truths. It is little inclined to examine what works; rather, it tends to criticize what does not. The problem is not that we have no examples of success, either in or out of government. There are, for instance, many programs to combat social problems such as drug abuse and alcoholism that are widely seen to work by conservatives and liberals alike. All of these programs have important lessons to offer. Yet they are treated as if they were all unique and non-replicable—if not inexplicable—with nothing to teach the larger society. The best known of these programs is Alcoholics Anonymous, but there are hundreds, if not thousands, of others organized on the same or analogous principles.

We ignore these programs in the larger policy debate because they operate without connection to our overcentralized national political culture. They involve local, self-governing institutions, in which people come together to find ways to address every kind of problem. These efforts succeed because of the dedication of people participating at the local level. There are only two possible ways for Washington to assist such efforts: first, to encourage a vision of a nation of engaged citizens, built from the bottom up; and second, to create policies and institutions that encourage such efforts and enable them to operate more easily—including policies to finance them.

Unfortunately, our politics is like a great theater; a spotlight shines on the great stage that is Washington, D.C. None of the major participants in the national political drama—not the "stars," not the "impresarios," not the "production crew," not the "theatrical critics"—have any interest in moving the spotlight to local and regional stages.

Our preoccupation with governing by exposing falsehood and understanding truth negatively underlies much of the sense of

breakdown in our politics. It stimulates and reinforces citizen alienation, which shows itself everywhere. Apart from consistent negative
response to surveys of attitudes toward politics, citizen alienation is
evident in the decline in voting, the weakening of political parties
(both in their role in government and in voter support), the reduction of participation in civic enterprises (especially community support of education), and the lack of popular willingness to pay for the
maintenance of public works.

Other signs of alienation are evident in the fact that although
voters regularly reelect almost all incumbent congressmen, the great
majority express little or no confidence in Congress.[1] Voters are
unyieldingly and overwhelmingly opposed to salary increases for
their representatives—even though inflation has greatly eroded
government salaries in real terms. It will be interesting, in the coming
years, to see if a constitutional amendment limiting the number of
terms a congressman can serve is passed—a proposal that has
strong public support.

These indicators of political crisis, which are almost universally
known, explain why a large majority of voters expresses profound
dissatisfaction with the state of U.S. politics.[2]

One major reason why citizens are so alienated is the growing
number of problems that government is apparently impotent to
solve. I cited a number of these in the prologue: homelessness and
the underclass, Wall Street cheating, rising crime levels, declining
educational achievement, worsening rates of drug and alcohol addiction, and many problems related to adolescent alienation, including disturbing increases in urban gang violence and suicide,
homicide, illegitimacy, and delinquency among the young. Our utter
incapacity to solve these problems highlights the perversity of our
indifference to citizen-led programs that have been demonstrated
not only to work, but to command admiration across the political
spectrum.

Studies of citizen alienation reveal another, even deeper reason
for disaffection. By a large majority, citizens feel that government is
not responsive to their needs. Most important, they feel that they are
not *involved.* They do not feel that their political representatives play
any positive role in empowering them to live the kinds of lives they
want to lead.

These complaints highlight the challenge of reconciling freedom
and order in politics. Modern people not only want to be free *from*

coercion; they also want to be free *to* control their own lives. They want to be self-governing—to control the principal institutions in their lives. This aspiration gave rise to the New Left's revolt against centralized institutions during the 1960s, and it is spreading throughout American society today.

These trends all underlie the antagonism people feel toward centralized politics. Unfortunately, neither of our major political parties has a convincing response.

The Centralization of the State

As I mentioned in Chapter 1, Jacob Burckhardt traced the origins of the modern state to the emergence of individualism in thirteenth-century Italy. Burckhardt emphasized the role of individualism in the appearance of the first traces of modern tyranny, in city-state regimes controlled by strong princes. The concurrent rise of individualism and the state is also connected to the emergence of reason and science, which aided the state in liberating and protecting individuals and securing their rights from strictures imposed by traditional moral and religious authorities.

Although the growth of the modern state has taken different paths in different countries, belief in the idealism associated with the centralized state has remained strong among "progressive" thinkers everywhere. This is true both in countries that were influenced by the ideas of the Anglo-Scottish Enlightenment—especially the United States and Britain—and in the countries that followed the more messianic tendencies in the French Enlightenment, which eventually produced modern socialism. In different ways, progressive thinkers everywhere continue to look to the state as the embodiment and exemplification of the highest aspirations and idealism of modern man. And since it is the left that has looked to the state for deliverance, the crisis of politics and the state is also the left's crisis.

Just as the rise of the state played an important role in setting individuals free, the search for a new form of order has in turn required rejection of the state's excesses.

These excesses were made most obvious in Marxism-Leninism, and it was in Marxist-Leninist states that the politics of the state failed most dramatically. The belief that the longing for a modern order could be realized by addressing a central problem (the class struggle) through the power of the state (the dictatorship of the proletariat) was mechanistic in the extreme. Like any machine, when Marxism failed, it could only do so completely—without the possibility of regeneration.

That it has certainly done. The social and economic crisis of Marxist countries everywhere has left no doubt as to its failure. The speed with which the former Soviet Union and countries in Eastern Europe have abandoned Marxism is astonishing. Despite the setback of Tiananmen Square, China already seems to have resumed its parallel course toward reform, at least in the economic realm.

Milder dependence on the state has also failed, however. Throughout the world, countries that have tried to realize equality by government fiat are in crisis, disrupted by underground economies, tax cheating, and emigration. I once heard the reply of a famous Soviet economist when he was asked if the Soviets were trying to emulate the Swedish economic model, with its commitment to social spending financed by very high tax rates: he quipped that he did not think it particularly healthy for a country to have all of its corporate leadership living in Switzerland. By defining the end of politics in terms of equality, Western liberals failed exactly where the Marxists failed.

But rejection of centralized, statist politics has not been limited to the political right. During the 1960s, the New Left rejected the rationalistic, mechanistic tendencies in modern progressive thought. It was then that the crisis we see all around us began—when conflict over the Vietnam War and race tore American society apart. Extreme, even authoritarian, actions and words became common on all sides of the debate. Epithets such as "pig" and "fascist" were staples in the vocabulary of aggression that replaced rational political debate. Calls to revolution were common on the left; the kinds of "dirty tricks" that culminated in Watergate were the right's principal venture in counterrevolution. Civility disappeared from political discourse, and it returned only after Watergate.

Although the New Left is no longer a strong political movement, its philosophy continues to have strong influence on the peace and environmentalist movements, and even on the understanding of what it means to be "disadvantaged" in our society. The legacy of the New Left, suspicion of centralized power both public and private, continues to be felt among freedom leftists; and if President Clinton tries to lead the United States into an increasingly state-centered politics, it is almost certain that a New Left will reappear in protest.

Whether the Clinton presidency adopts a statist position will depend largely on whether the order left has changed in recent decades. In the postwar era the order left led the United States and other Western democracies to embrace the centralized state in a much milder form than did the Marxist countries. At any rate, the *means* used by the Western state were milder. The important question, however, is whether the *ends* it sought were any less absolute. In the future, will the commitment to equality of the order left in power yield at any point to other, competing values? If it does not, then it seems likely that President Clinton will move strongly to use federal action to pursue order liberalism's customary social and political ends.

Irving Kristol once wrote an essay that may shed some light on the issue. He puzzled over why left-liberal egalitarians refused to delimit the optimal amount of equality in a liberal democracy.[3] He wrote, for example, of his repeated attempts to encourage leading liberals to specify a society's ideal income distribution. Lester Thurow finally took up the challenge, but in the end pronounced his own proposed standard as only an "interim equity target"—implying that a more fundamental goal lay beyond it.[4]

Thurow failed to conclude that the left's commitment to equality had any limits at all. The difficulties in setting such a limit, combined with growing signs of breakdown in centralized politics, counsel pessimism for those who look to a renewed reliance on federal power to accomplish their purposes.

The Breakdown of Centralized Politics

The left's tenacity in pursuing equality in politics is one reason why our politics remains so polarized. The restoration of calm in the 1970s was not complete. The distrust between political opponents that was pervasive during the 1960s has recently been made evident again in the controversy over Irangate, in the tone of the Senate confirmation hearings on the nominations of Robert Bork and Clarence Thomas to serve on the U.S. Supreme Court, and in the continuing practice at universities of shouting down speakers with unpopular messages. It is also evident on the right, with disruptive political demonstrations against abortion and (at the 1992 Republican convention) for "family values."

The extraordinary collapse of communism in the former Soviet Union and the Eastern bloc countries temporarily diverted our attention from these troubles; but in the recent presidential election campaign, commentators of all political stripes resumed their partisan bickering. In this overheated atmosphere President Bush's popularity fell from all-time highs after the Gulf War to all-time lows.

The political winds are filled with criticism, both from the left and the right; yet both sides issue only high-minded calls to do more of what has been shown to fail. Lacking a principle of order and obligation that is consistent with our commitment to individual freedom, both conservatives and liberals call for reform in familiar ways: conservatives argue for less government; liberals call for more.* President Reagan, for example, led an extraordinary counterattack against the growth of the federal government but provided little leadership in developing the local public and private self-governing institutions that would resuscitate our deteriorating political and social life. Reagan's was a negative vision in important respects; President Bush substantially continued Reagan's program with even less positive vision.

Order liberals retreat to ideas they call "progressive," but that are in fact only repackaged versions of outmoded involuntary concepts of order. Although Bill Clinton showed signs at the Democratic convention of wanting to move in new directions, in the campaign he returned to the safety of centralized politics. He, like other Democratic leaders, had to mollify powerful political constituencies that have no interest in or understanding of citizens' desire for more control over their own lives. Feminism, environmentalism, and other, similar movements offer new versions of socialism's characteristic tendency to coerce behavior through the power of the government.

New liberal and Democratic party groups constantly appear, seeking to lead the party away from this tendency. But it is hard for them to succeed because the Democrats are the reflexive party of Washington, D.C.—heirs to the modernist belief in the centralized

---

*Again, conservatives are divided into freedom and order tendencies, as are liberals. But lacking any way of integrating these ideas, their superior functions push the former toward freedom, the latter toward order.

state—and their mainly liberal leadership knows only how to impose more taxes, more spending, and more regulation of our economic and social life. While liberals accuse Republicans and conservatives of promoting the interests of the rich, liberals are no less handmaidens of their own self-interested constituencies. As each election day approaches, Democratic presidential candidates return to the populism of another era; and their inability to escape from this and move on explains why it is so hard for the Democrats to win presidential elections. I say this notwithstanding the results of the 1992 presidential election. What defeated President Bush was a sluggish economy, caused in substantial part by a disastrously restrictive monetary policy over the two years preceding the election. If the economy had continued the strong recovery that the Federal Reserve aborted in the spring of 1991, there can be little doubt that President Bush would have won a landslide reelection.

I might mention that although it is extremely difficult for the Democratic party to wean itself from centralized politics, there are important signs that elements of the intellectual left are moving rapidly in that direction. As I have already noted, the spring 1992 issue of the leftist journal *Telos* is devoted entirely to an embrace of federalist decentralization.

The only way out of this dilemma lies in the search to discover a politics that integrates freedom and order. That means building institutions at the local level that allow citizens the sense of involvement, participation, and self-governance that they cannot find in politics centralized in Washington. This would produce the political synthesis of freedom and order that is crucial to the intellectual coherence of our entire political enterprise.

Apart from the reluctance of Washington-based politicians and media people to give up center stage, there is an important philosophical reason why Democrats and Republicans, liberals and conservatives, have not provided the leadership we need to accomplish this self-governing vision. For Democrats and liberals, focused on state-imposed equality and community, the problem has been a lack of confidence that people can be self-governing and work voluntarily for the common good. Republicans and conservatives, on the other hand, are so focused on freedom from government that they have not worked for self-governance either.

So long as these two positions dominate our major political parties, the crisis in our politics will continue.

Rethinking Politics

We must undertake a fundamental rethinking of our politics. Such a rethinking is crucial now, as geopolitical changes suggest a radical reduction of the state's original central function, national defense. Although liberals in the United States hope that reduced military spending will make possible a "peace dividend" that will allow increased government funding of social programs, the opposite may well happen. The decline in the government's geopolitical function may well accelerate voters' declining confidence and interest in the federal government. This may leave little public appetite for any ambitious expansion of what many voters see as failed federal programs.

Order liberalism finds itself in crisis for the same reasons, in general, that order conservatism does: because each, unable to incorporate the human impulse to seek freedom, ultimately retreats and embraces a coercive order to further its ends. Each sees opposition to its policies not as a demand for freedom but as an ominous rejection of its values. Each concludes, therefore, that society must "go back." Order conservatives say that society must go back to the traditions of the past; order liberals say the state must break up and destroy the oppressive effects of tradition, restoring society to its original humanness. Both visions treat citizens as children, treat their demands for the freedom to make their own commitments to responsibility as hugely mistaken.

The social problems that are the concern of the order left are troublesome and real, and they deserve serious attention. But solutions will require far more dedication than can be provided by government spending alone. Social critics on the left often excoriate Americans for believing they can buy anything with money. But the same misconception also applies to social problems: we cannot buy solutions to these, either. Thinking we can trivializes the problems; a much deeper approach is required.

Liberals have never viewed aggrandizement of the state as an end; they have seen it as a means to liberate the individual, releasing him from the false consciousness rooted in tradition. But after two centuries of experimentation with state intervention to solve social problems, it is clear that, although tradition continues its decline, the state shows no signs of withering away in response. The state has

become an increasingly decadent political form, whose only end is
its own perpetuation.

Belief in the redemptive state rests on confidence that those who
run it—both elected politicians and bureaucrats—are somehow
immune from the false consciousness that afflicts less enlightened
members of society. This is, of course, a mistake. Although great
statesmen do appear from time to time, their appearance is unpre-
dictable. In general, public officials and politicians are no better—
no less corruptible—than those they govern. And especially in this
age of television, the personal qualities that get politicians elected
are not often those that enable them to lead us out of our social
dilemma. Since politicians are certainly corruptible by power, corruption has become an increasing problem as power has become
more centralized. The effect of this intensifying power explains how
centralized governments become what political theorist Vincent Ostrom calls "predatory states," encouraging "rent-seeking"—
profiteering—by elites with access to political power.[5]

The limitations of policy and opinion makers informs a larger
principle of political behavior that is analogous to an important tenet
of modern physics. One of the chief assumptions of Newtonian
physics—the physics before Einstein and quantum mechanics—
was that the world (phenomena) exists independent of anyone
observing it. Modern physics, on the other hand, takes as one of its
starting assumptions that observers of natural phenomena must regard *themselves* as an integral part of what they are observing.

I believe the same must be true in understanding the crisis in our
politics: in considering solutions, we must include the influence of
principal observers of our politics—policy makers, academics,
media people, and other opinion-making groups—in any possible
solution. This is important for two reasons: first, because these
groups dominate both the political and moral idioms of modern,
communication-based society; and second, because they themselves reflect, in their personal lives, the major elements that underlie
our larger moral and social breakdown.

It remains hard for us, as citizens of a democracy, to see the
challenge that is upon us. Francis Fukuyama's celebrated and con-
troversial essay "The End of History?" argues that the victory of
liberal democracy over Marxism has brought the evolution of political thinking to an end.[6] The debate that followed only showed how
hard it is for us to see the frailties of liberal democracy: almost none
of the disputants warned of any threat to democratic institutions.

Because the claims of liberal democracy are more moderate than those of Marxism, its failings are harder to see, and its decline and vulnerability remain largely hidden from us.

Before the emergence of Soviet *perestroika,* all major political positions in the West could define themselves in relation to Marxism—conservatives opposing it as the enemy of everything good, and liberals and leftists embracing many of its ends, if not its means. Each group either repudiated or aped the methods of Marxism, so as to avoid developing its own solutions to the problems of our society. Today, however, we must look to ourselves.

The decline of the federal role in international relations will accentuate the crisis in our politics, but it will also offer us a great opportunity to resolve our dilemma. To do so, however, will require a fundamental rethinking of our purposes and possibilities. There are signs that such a rethinking may be in the offing. Continuing political breakdown and alienation may force us to it sooner than we think.

How can the problem of centralized power be resolved? If top-down, centralized politics does not work, what alternative is there? How can we build new kinds of institutions that leave people free from coercive power and free to work cooperatively with others— thus helping to integrate freedom and order in both individuals and society?

The Rediscovery of Self-Governance

Any serious plan for renewal must include institutions that empower citizens to participate in and govern all public institutions that are essentially local in nature. An important element of such institutions is that participation must be voluntary. People must be able to leave, to opt out, to seek alternatives, if they feel institutions are not meeting their needs—whether in housing, education, or other areas of their life. When laws and constitutional rules encourage and expand individual choices and opportunities for participation in governance, citizens at all levels of society are freed to contribute in a multitude of ways to economic and social progress. When they narrow or even deny choices, the effect can be to exclude a large fraction of a country's citizens from participating in its formal (as opposed to informal or underground) economic and social activities.

Self-governance depends on the idea that people should govern their own lives—that their doing so is good in itself, independent of questions of efficiency. It views inputs (human effort) as having a nonmaterial, even spiritual, worth. This allows self-governance to value both inputs and outputs independently; it allows one to see the contributions of, say, a bank president and a gardener as equal in some fundamental sense.

I use the word "subjective" to describe this nonmaterial standard of value. Since this word will play a vital role in this book, it is important that I define it clearly. In the broadest sense, subjectivity describes reality as perceived: a person's internal world; his beliefs, attitudes, and feelings. In contrast, "objectivity" refers to reality independent of the mind: that which is external to each person. In the thesis I argue here—that the major force driving our crisis of values is the broad advance of consciousness of the individual self—subjectivity also connotes the dilemma of individualistic man, increasingly imprisoned in his interior life, seeking a way to reengage with his objective surroundings: with society, the world, and the cosmos.

In the sense in which I use it, subjectivity does not necessarily refer to emotions and feelings. Rather, it implies a growing consciousness of self that is expanding people's need to exercise control over their own lives, both individual and political. My dominant interest, therefore, is in how we can engage the subjective consciousness to establish a sense of personal control over our existence.

The self-governing model appreciates value at two levels. One is tangible, objective, economic; the other is intangible, subjective, and human. This two-dimensional value system underlies the self-governing approach to the world, which borrows the best of both capitalism and socialism and combines them in an integrated vision. It celebrates both the capitalist commitment to individual freedom and the socialist commitment to cooperation and community.

Although the Western democracies have well-developed market economies that encourage entrepreneurship in private profit-making activities, political power has been concentrated in the central state. All Western countries, for instance, are characterized by a strong bias in favor of centralized political direction of social services—from schools to public housing to legal services. This bias has greatly limited citizen participation in real self-governance. Fortunately, signs of change are appearing.

A Problem with Two Dimensions

The problem of moving to a new kind of politics, grounded in the self-governance of individuals and communities, has two dimensions. One is objective and tangible and has an institutional solution: it is concerned with achieving an end. The other dimension is subjective: it is focused primarily on the means to that end—on a change in the *spirit* of individuals and the community that comprises them. The ultimate challenge to the creation of a really new conception of politics is whether people can embrace, for themselves and for others, the idea of participation, both subjective and objective, that is the heart of self-governance.

The objective, institutional dimension of establishing such a new politics is relatively straightforward and (assuming the will to do it) easy to implement. It requires radical decentralization of government functions.* I focus here on expanding choice, and on trusting people to reach out voluntarily to each other and cooperate in a common enterprise.

The subjective, conceptual dimension is more difficult to comprehend, because it requires transcendence of the modernist focus on the objective, to an appreciation of the subjective as having at least coequal value. Understanding the subjective dimension, however, should not be as difficult as it was even two decades ago, because growing numbers of progressive movements—beginning with environmentalism and now including most efforts on behalf of the disadvantaged—are focusing less on material (objective) problems, such as simple poverty, and more on nonmaterial (subjective) problems.

---

*Decentralization can and should also occur in private organizations, especially in large, centralized corporations. I have emphasized the government here because, in its traditional mode, it is explicitly and inherently monopolistic, offering no alternatives and therefore no choice.

6

The Social
Agenda

There are many theories about why an advanced industrial democracy such as the United States continues to have serious social problems. These problems are symbolized by the extraordinary numbers of the dispossessed homeless, wandering our city streets as haunted nomads. Although both the left and right express strong views about this situation, few on either side are confident they really know what is wrong or what to do about it.

The differences between liberal and conservative views on the subject are well known. Liberals argue that the underclass lacks such things as affordable housing and jobs, which they believe the government should provide. Conservatives, on the other hand, think the underclass lacks other kinds of resources—motivation, knowledge, market opportunities—which are difficult for others to provide. Conservatives believe that governments actively make social problems worse—either directly by promoting welfare dependency, or indirectly by maintaining legal barriers that discourage people from undertaking productive economic activity. Beyond that, conservatives look to local organizations and communities, especially the family, to support members of the underclass and motivate them to join the economic and social mainstream.

The differences between these positions are well known, but the similarities between them are more interesting.

The most important similarity is that both sides see social problems in essentially objective terms. That is, both believe that the problems have primarily objective causes and can be solved by objective, institutional reforms. Tax policy, income redistribution, and the opening of market opportunities are all examples of objective means that liberals and conservatives rely on in addressing the issue of poverty.

Although most observers limit themselves to the objective dimension, one group, primarily composed of conservatives, believes that the overriding issue in addressing poverty is the problem of *character*.[1]

I will argue that people in the United States and Western Europe worry far more about both inequality and social problems than do people in India and China, where poverty and inequality are objectively much greater problems. This suggests that more than simply objective factors are involved. The reason for the difference is that equality is a subjective, individualistic value, of much greater concern to a modern society like the United States than to traditional societies such as China and India.[2] Inequality is seen as a problem mainly by individualistic societies because it is in those societies that individuals experience shame at being poor.

This point explains an important part of the reason most socialist countries are ultimately unable to achieve equality or solve related social problems—because they are modern, not traditional, societies. Evidence from the former Soviet Union and Eastern Europe, until recently Marxist, suggests that these countries suffer even greater inequality and crises of values than do the countries of the West. If China seems to be without the tensions associated with poverty and inequality, it is more because China is traditional than because it is communist.

We Americans will not begin to correct any of our major social problems until we fundamentally reorient the way we think. To make real progress, we must move beyond our mechanistic, objective view of social problems and consider subjective issues as well.

Coming to terms with the subjective will change more than our approach to the problems of the disadvantaged. If the people who formulate our current understanding of social problems would include *themselves* in their observations of our political and social life, they would see a crucial piece of the puzzle that is now hidden from them. I am referring to intellectuals—writers, artists, social scientists, and policy makers—the people who shape social values through their control of the intellectual and moral idiom.

In this chapter, I will make an argument that takes account of both traditional conservatives' concern about the influence of character on social problems and order liberals' analysis of the causes of poverty and inequality. But my argument will depart from theirs in small but crucial ways.

I will argue that increasing individualism and people's related dependence on publicly recognized rewards as affirmations of self-worth are the major causes of modern social problems. I will also argue that solving social problems will require reducing the importance of those rewards. In the past, socialists have tried to accomplish this with government policies that take rewards (especially money and other status symbols) away from people. Such policies have failed. The reason for this is that social problems can only be solved by addressing their internal, subjective aspects; they cannot be solved by means such as high taxes, which affect only their objective manifestations.

I will argue that the importance of externally bestowed rewards can only be reduced by a rediscovery of meaning and purpose beyond the self—a system of meaning whose appeal is such as to encourage voluntary commitment. As with the problem of reconciling the values of capitalism and socialism, therefore, reducing inequality will depend, finally, on our finding a way to integrate freedom and order. And the most difficult challenge in accomplishing this objective will be changing the attitudes of intellectuals themselves, since they are the thought-leaders who are responsible for our increasing reliance on external rewards for affirmation of individual identity.

To examine these propositions in light of the current policy debate, let us begin by reviewing how aid programs for the disadvantaged over the past three decades have shifted their objectives from practical ends, which could be realized by policy, to goals impossible to satisfy. There have been three shifts in our concerns: from absolute poverty to relative poverty, from equal opportunity to equal results, and from equality for individuals to equality for groups. Understanding why the newer objectives are beyond the capacity of any policy to accomplish will set the stage for examining the problem of equality in a new way.

From Absolute to Relative Deprivation

Until relatively recently, concern about equality focused on objective poverty. This concern was particularly (and legitimately) strong in the nineteenth century and again during the Great Depression. Throughout the nineteenth century, reformers focused on relieving absolute deprivation, improving working conditions, and alleviating the hardships and social dislocations that attended the early stages of industrial capitalism.

Through the end of the nineteenth century and into the twentieth, society got richer and the hardships declined. In terms of official 1989 standards of poverty (an income of $12,675 in 1987 dollars for a nonfarm family of four), 90 percent of the U.S. population was poor in 1900. The number fell to 50 percent by 1920, and to 20 percent in 1962. In 1989 the figure was 12.8 percent.

This improving picture probably explains why Charles Murray, in his book *Losing Ground: America's Social Policy 1950–1980,* found no concern about poverty or social justice in America expressed in the leading popular magazines of the early 1950s—*Time, Life, Newsweek, Colliers,* and others. Even the liberal *New Republic,* which in a special midcentury "State of the Union" editorial referred to the "10 million American families who earn less than $2,000" a year, made no urgent call for reform. Considering that about forty-five million Americans, or in 1950 about 30 percent of the population, were poor by present-day standards, the lack of solicitude seems astonishing.

But as the number of poor continued to decline, concern began to shift. The focus on ameliorating poverty initially gave way to a desire to ensure equal opportunity, first through equal enforcement of rights under the law, later by establishing a basic "floor" of material conditions beneath which people would not be permitted to fall.

In the early 1960s, the publication of Michael Harrington's *The Other America* stimulated a changed perception. The new attention focused on the so-called cycle of poverty, wherein a large underclass was found to be caught in chronic distress, sometimes for generation after generation. During President Kennedy's short administration, plans were thus developed for a major new government initiative to fight poverty. This was finally implemented in 1964 as President Johnson's Great Society programs.

Past efforts had been formulated to create opportunities by providing basic material aid in the form of housing and jobs, and later to eliminate legal obstacles to opportunity. Their focus was entirely on changing external, objective conditions. In the 1960s, on the other hand, the people who designed such Great Society programs as Head Start set out to eliminate the subjective obstacles to opportunity as well. They aimed quite explicitly to change poor people's internal attitudes. They tried to counter and correct cultural deprivation in the early years of life, as well as to give disadvantaged people real control over their own lives

By the end of the decade, the Great Society programs had failed to achieve the progress hoped for, and demands began to be heard to guarantee equality of achievement, not just of opportunity. The commitment to this new kind of equality was most evident in expansion of the concept of affirmative action to include "commercial goals and timetables," or job quotas, as provided for in federal guidelines promulgated in December 1971.[3] In the late 1960s and early 1970s, however, the principle of affirmative action provided the authority for a series of court decisions that imposed increasingly stringent obligations on employers to hire minority-group members and women. These led in turn to the setting of quotas, organized by racial and sexual category, in employment and education. The new commitment to enforced equality thus marked a shift from the attempt to aid individuals to an effort to improve the lot of entire population groups.

The commitment to guarantee equality of living standards was part of an emerging concern about relative deprivation. More than thirty years ago, in *The Affluent Society,* John Kenneth Galbraith stated the problem as follows:

> People are poverty-stricken when their income, even if adequate for survival, falls markedly behind that of the community. Then they cannot have what the larger community regards as the minimum necessary for decency; and they cannot wholly escape, therefore, the judgment of the larger community that they are indecent. They are degraded for, in the literal sense, they live outside the grades or categories which the community regards as acceptable.[4]

Galbraith was writing about the problem of relative income: those who end up at the bottom, those who feel like (and are regarded as) failures, become likely candidates to suffer social problems such as homelessness or drug addiction.

Relative poverty is regarded as a problem mainly in modern, individualistic societies, which tend to motivate their members with external rewards. The greater the importance of such rewards, the greater the sense of defeat and shame for those who end up at the bottom for whatever reason. Liberals focus on this problem in advancing the cause of disadvantaged groups, such as blacks and women, whose average incomes are below national levels, and who are often underrepresented in higher-status occupations.

As concern has shifted from absolute to relative poverty, and from guaranteeing opportunity to guaranteeing equality, a third shift in policy emphasis has also occurred: moving away from concern about equality for individuals to equality for groups.

From Individual to Group Equality

In the past two decades concern about the representation of racial, ethnic, and sexual groups in employment has motivated growing support for the idea of economic equality for groups. There has been a corresponding, necessary abandonment of the long-held commitment to individual opportunity. The enormity of this shift has largely escaped serious debate, but it is affecting large numbers of young people especially, who are discovering that the world does not always offer rewards commensurate with effort. It remains to be seen how this ultimately affects American society, but the magnitude of the change will probably be enormous.

There are great opportunities for confusion to arise between the established commitment to individuals and the new concern for groups. Many real conflicts are already evident in policy. One example is the contradiction between efforts to open opportunities for minority-group members' success in the larger society and simultaneous efforts (through bilingual education and other means) to protect distinct minority-group cultures, even if those cultures may retard material achievement among their members.

American society today ensures equality of individual opportunity by reliance on external rewards—that is, rewards that improve one's standing relative to others. Success is thus achieved only by acquiring money, status, or power—not other, internally appreciated rewards, such as leisure or love. In the policy debate about equality, internal rewards are considered to have no value in measuring success. As a result, government policies aimed at ensuring equality concentrate on equalizing opportunity to acquire only external rewards.

A system that emphasizes external rewards tends to be understood as a zero-sum game. Only 10 percent of a population can rank in the top 10 percent of that population in terms of income, status, or educational scores. If someone improves his position and moves into the top 10 percent, it can only be because someone else moves down. Yet public discussions of these issues seem vaguely to assume that if we all only tried a little harder, if only we could muster additional goodwill and idealism, everyone could be "above average" in everything worth having or doing.

In his book *Making It,* Norman Podhoretz recalls from childhood his awareness of achievement judged in this way:

> [O]n the surface the "gospel of success" did reign supreme in the world of my childhood. Success did not necessarily, or even primarily, mean money; just as often it might mean prestige or popularity. In any case, the concept always referred . . . to *the possession of goods which had value in the eyes of others.* These goods might also have had value in one's own eyes, but that was a secondary consideration, if indeed it was ever considered at all. The main thing was to be *esteemed.*[5]

Achievement, that is, was to be accomplished to impress others, not to satisfy oneself. By this externalized standard, in order for there to be winners there must also be relative losers; and the losers are those at the bottom, who feel the shame and humiliation of their station. In a competition for external rewards, somebody must always end up at the bottom and "fail."

The increasing organization of society according to external standards does provide opportunities for individual success. But the necessary, relative failure of other people creates concern that entire population groups may be failing. Liberals and conservatives alike value both opportunities for individuals and the sense of community provided by traditional societies—the first representing freedom, the second representing order. Both liberals and conservatives, however, are uncertain and ambivalent about how to reconcile the contradictory claims that inevitably arise between these positions.

Liberals, for instance, act as steadfast proponents of equal valuation of groups when they question the superiority of Western, modernist culture. What right, liberals often ask, do we have to assert the superiority of our culture over others? They express this pluralistic perspective in their commitment to programs for bilingual education and to a general belief that minority groups should be encouraged to maintain and preserve their "cultural heritage." This view has at times taken an extreme form, in calls for recognition of "black English" as separate but equal to the English spoken and written by the mainstream (white) culture.

But liberals also support equality of opportunity for individuals, which cuts in the opposite direction—toward intolerance of traditional, premodern values when these are seen as being at odds with the mainstream culture. Equal opportunity, after all, must include the freedom to escape a restrictive minority-group culture; to leave an Indian reservation (say) and seek wealth and status in the larger society.

Conservatives are no less ambivalent. On the one hand, they criticize bilingual education and the equal regard for non-Western cultures as likely to retard individual achievement. Anyone hoping to become a bank president, they argue, will require at a minimum the ability to speak the same English as the bank's clients. Encouraging people to think otherwise simply puts them at a disadvantage, and hence deprives them of opportunities.

Yet conservatives also support community and group values. They credit traditional and religious ethics for supplying the "spiritual and moral capital" that sustains a liberal, individualistic society. They also subscribe to the pluralist values that Nathan Glazer and Daniel P. Moynihan observed in their 1963 classic, *Beyond the Melting Pot,* which studied how five ethnic and racial groups in New York City maintained identities separate and distinct from the mainstream city culture.

At the end of the 1960s conservatives hoped that the black power movement might come to reflect some genuinely positive group values. And they still hope that such a spirit may encourage black and Hispanic communities to develop their own, more workable alternatives to the state-sponsored educational system.

Although the ideals of individual opportunity and group identity often conflict, most intellectuals on both left and right embrace both, without attempting to resolve the conflict. This is because neither left nor right has reconciled its own commitments to freedom and order.

At a large dinner gathering of New York intellectuals that I attended some years ago, I began to wonder if intellectuals were not the chief "carriers" and proponents of the external standard. During casual conversation several of the guests expressed wonder that the great majority of people, who would never enjoy the success that these intellectuals had, could avoid seeing their meager lives as failures. If intellectuals do believe this (and I think they generally do), it is because the external standard comes closer to describing *their* lives and the way they define themselves than it does the lives of most people. Yet most intellectuals claim to reject the pursuit of external rewards as vulgar.

For most people who think seriously about it, a system focused only on external rewards is absurd, because it does not include many of the things that motivate most people. Most of us live our lives and measure success and failure in a way that combines external and internal rewards. Beyond being absurd, the narrower standard carries the dismaying implication that the whole of life—all that we live for—can (or should) be measured by an external standard.

Fortunately, a very different kind of achievement is also possible: an internal or private standard of excellence, which means doing one's best, regardless of comparisons with others. By this way of reckoning, "winners" and "losers" win or lose only in relation to themselves. This standard does not involve a zero-sum game; everybody has a chance to win. It is this concept that is behind the old saying, "It doesn't matter whether you win or lose, it's how you play the game." Unfortunately, the irony with which this saying is regarded today reveals the power of the other, external definition of achievement. Moreover, I believe the power of the external standard is growing.

Inequality and Social Problems

Perhaps the most persistent social problem in the United States is the existence of an apparently permanent underclass, marked by the demoralization of its members, who feel locked into failure, without hope.

During the 1970s a lively debate raged over explanations of the "irresponsible" behavior identified with lower-class culture and the so-called culture of poverty. This behavior includes the widespread failure to establish steady work habits—and thus to hold regular employment—and the disinclination to defer gratification, which results in an inability to save money.[6] The debate in the 1970s focused on causes: whether this behavior is primarily *socialized* into the culture of the lower class or whether it is an *adaptive response* to a life without meaningful opportunities. If the first explanation were true, members of the underclass would not be expected to respond to changes in objective circumstances stimulated by policy. If the second were correct, they would respond if policy could improve their opportunities.[7] Order conservatives favor the first hypothesis, liberals and freedom conservatives the second. To the extent order conservatives are correct that the problem is endemic to lower-class culture, there is little we can do. To the extent the problem is a lack of opportunity—a view I hold, in at least some degree—we can have hope. The views of both left and right on strategies for enlarging opportunity are well known. I want here to examine a different interpretation of equality and opportunity—and a different strategy for solving social problems that arises from it.

This new interpretation of the dilemma of the underclass should become clear if we compare two hypothetical societies, each occupying a remote island, and each consisting of three people.

On the first island the inhabitants have developed an extraordinarily simple and crude status system based on only a single external value. That value is height: the tallest person has the most status, the next tallest is in the middle, and the shortest is at the bottom. All three people are fully grown, so there is no chance that the shortest will ever be anywhere but at the bottom: there are no opportunities for social mobility on the island.

How will this system affect the three island inhabitants? How will it affect their self-images and identities? Will this small society have a "culture of poverty" and an underclass? Will the shortest among them take on the characteristics we associate with lower-class culture—becoming present-oriented, unable to defer gratification, feeling defeated and ashamed to be at the bottom? Will he regard his life as a failure?

The answer to these questions depends almost certainly on how important status is to the person who is shortest. And that will depend, at least in part, on how important it is to the rest of the island's mini-society. The more important status is, the more the shortest will regard his life as a failure, and the more likely he will become the island's "underclass." The less important it is to him, the less he will fear failure, and the more equal he will feel, seeking value in pleasures other than improvement in status. In the latter case, the value system will likely feature internal rewards, and he will be able to feel genuinely equal to the others, although he will recognize his individual difference. The social hierarchy will not be a zero-sum game.

This example shows, I think, why modern, individualistic societies such as the United States tend to be far more concerned about equality than are traditional societies—which is why a society like communist China can seem extremely egalitarian even as it is rigidly hierarchical. Our mythical island, which is very different from twentieth-century America, reveals a paradox: rigid hierarchical societies that offer little or no opportunity for upward (or downward) mobility often emphasize internal rewards and therefore tend to be freer of class conflict than societies which, like ours, allow much greater mobility. The reason people in individualistic societies worry about equality is that their greater opportunity for external rewards makes the struggle for such rewards more contentious. In societies with fixed social positions, like our island, the absence of opportunity for changed status tends to make success and status matters of less concern. Since the sense of failure can only be as powerful as the drive for success, there will be little fear of failure—and therefore no culture of poverty. But again, only a nonindividualistic society could have such a system.

These factors explain why the leftists who have idealized traditional and tribal societies frequently have not resented the hierarchical nature of those societies. Perhaps the most extreme example of this was the belief, widely held by leftists, especially in the 1960s, that China was egalitarian. Hoover Institution sociologist Alex Inkeles tells a story about an experience he had in China that exposes the reality of conditions there. When Inkeles was served tea one afternoon, his wife got only hot water, because she was assumed to have far lower status than he. China's extreme inequality is even more horrifyingly indicated by its high incidence of infanticide of female babies, reflecting deep-seated beliefs about the inferiority of women.

Now let's move to another hypothetical island, which is also occupied by three people. This second group has developed a status system based not on height, but weight: the heaviest person has the most status, and the thinnest, the least. All three have almost identical frames on which to develop pounds, so it is never certain who will have the most status on any given day.

The second island is more akin to the United States today. As on the first island, people living on the second will respond to the status system to a degree that depends on how important status is to them. But on the second island, each person has almost total freedom and opportunity to become number one at any time, if he only eats enough. The opportunity for mobility (external rewards) on the second island is virtually unlimited.

What can we say about the second island society? What can we say about the likelihood that it will place great value on external rewards? We can say that the chances are very good it will. We do not know, of course: the existence of a temptation does not mean people will succumb to it. We *can* say that to the extent the people on the second island think success is important, the opportunity for mobility will create uncertainty, perhaps unbearable anxiety, fears of failure and impotence, and so on. *And that will be true as much for the person who is number one as it is for the person who is number three.* In fact, fear of failure and apprehension about the future may become so intense on the second island that conceivably all three people would live present-oriented lives of the sort characterizing the "culture of poverty." (Think of the high-paid executives in our society who are addicted to drugs.)

Comparing these two islands affords us a way of looking at social change in many parts of the world, as increasing individualism has everywhere tended to push societies from the situation on the first island toward that on the second. It is the move from a world of tradition, emphasizing group values and internal rewards, to today's celebration of individual freedom and external prizes. Of course, every effort to extend opportunity for mobility has tended to escalate the emphasis on success, achievement, and status. As the emphasis on success has increased, so has anxiety, for rich and poor alike. This may explain a great deal about why members of the counterculture, who have come furthest along the path of individualism, often celebrate the culture of American Indians and other nonindividualistic, even tribal societies.

What do these examples suggest about our society today, our

cities filled with homeless people? Comparing the two hypothetical islands indicates the potential for a revised concept of opportunity, which may be more important than the conventional sort to empowering the underclass: opportunity created by social norms that emphasize internal values. The availability of this deeper kind of opportunity depends on moderating the stress that society and culture place on externalized notions of success and achievement. The greater that emphasis, the more it will paralyze people—and, paradoxically, limit their "opportunities" for achievement.

As we saw on the second island, the more important achieve ment and success are, the more people, at both the top and the bottom, will fear the future. The more anxiety-ridden the achievement of success is, the more failure will haunt those at the bottom; and the more the *fear* of failure will haunt those at the top. In both cases, these rules apply even more to children than to adults.

Why "Social Action" and Political Reforms Cannot Work

This discussion suggests why any strategy that seeks to bolster equality solely through government action is doomed to fail. Limits on the success any citizen can enjoy fail because they treat only symptoms. When the underlying problem is the desire of individuals to distinguish themselves through the accumulation of external rewards (especially money), proponents of government intervention respond by trying to take away the rewards (especially by taxes). Since they have done nothing to get at the cultural motivation underlying the problem, they only encourage the emergence of black markets, tax dodges, and other means of subversion. If people want to differentiate themselves, they will find a way to do it.

If anything, policy interventions will become even more hopeless in the future, as the advance of individualism continues. Recognition of this appears to be increasing in many countries, as tax rates are being reduced, and command-and-control regulations have largely fallen into disrepute.[8]

A deeper reason why government action fails and will continue to fail derives from the phenomenon of poverty as a relative problem. If inequality comes from the desire of people to differentiate themselves, then as long as that desire remains, those at the bottom of society will perceive themselves as losers no matter how policy makers try to manipulate the terms of differentiation. In questioning the efficacy of government programs to redistribute income, Harvard philosopher Robert Nozick has argued that, while lessening income differences may reduce the importance of income in distinguishing people, if the need to compete remains, other externalized differences will only become more important.[9] Beauty? Brains? No matter the standard chosen, there will still be winners and losers—and still a lower class. There will still be social problems: the problems that characteristically afflict the demoralized underclass.

A culture of poverty and all related social problems will thus persist in spite of government programs to alleviate them. In fact, it is possible that the harder society tries to solve these problems politically, the more it is likely both to reflect and to encourage the perception that external rewards are all that matter. If this happens, the problems will only worsen.

If all of this is true, what can we do about it? Before we address that huge question, let us at least note that we cannot begin to understand our dilemma until we understand the full extent to which the custodians of our intellectual discourse—intellectuals themselves—are implicated in it.

Why Intellectuals Are Driven by External Rewards

Intellectuals are important here because, although they pretend otherwise, they are the group in society most active in promoting the importance of external rewards. And they do this because, more than almost any other group, they depend on such rewards for their self-definition. This was a central point in Norman Podhoretz's *Making It:* that ambition—the longing for wealth, power, and especially fame—is replacing sex "as the prime dirty little secret of the well-educated American soul." The dinner conversation I witnessed among the New York intelligentsia was not an aberration.

The currency intellectuals most value is recognition. The truth of this claim is indicated by the rash of news stories several years ago revealing that scholars at even the most prestigious research universities have been caught phonying their research findings.

Tom Wolfe has done more than anyone to chronicle how the

upper-middle-class intelligentsia manifests its anxious, "radical-chic" status mongering.[10] He describes how moneyed patrons of modern art in the 1960s used their hobby to take the sting out of wealth and distinguish themselves from the middle class:

> See? I'm not like *them*—those Jaycees, those United Fund chairmen, those Young Presidents, those mindless New York A. C. *goyisheh* hog-jowled stripe-tied goddamn-good-to-see-you-you-old-bastard-you oyster-bar trenchermen. . . . Avant-garde art, more than any other, takes the Mammon and the Moloch out of money, puts Levi's, turtlenecks, muttonchops, and other mantles and laurels of bohemian grace upon it.[11]

Wolfe's satire, while sharp, occasionally hits easy targets. If he really wanted to identify the most achievement-obsessed people, those whose lust for fame rather than money is strongest, he should have made the central character in his 1987 novel *The Bonfire of the Vanities* a power-hungry journalist instead of a pedestrian Wall Street bond salesman.

In *Making It,* Podhoretz exalts the quest for fame over the pursuit of money. Fame, he says, quoting Milton, is the calling of poets. Burckhardt associated the modern idea of fame with the appearance of the individual at the end of the Middle Ages.[12] Its "first witness" was Dante, who affirmed its emptiness while still longing for it.

Fame is the highest calling of intellectuals because recognition is the ultimate confirmation of achievement, the ultimate external confirmation. Money is a secondary concern for people truly possessed by the need to impress others. Nor is power without fame worth much. Fame, after all, is a more purely external prize—for it lacks all meaning or worth apart from its impact on others.

Why, if liberal intellectuals are so absorbed by external rewards, do they spend such energy belittling them? The answer is this: it is precisely their enslavement by the need to be recognized that makes intellectuals so ambivalent about external rewards. In his exploration of what he calls "the shadow," Jung recalled the old saying: "You are what you behold, and you behold what you are." People see themselves in others. What is more, people like and dislike most in others what they like and dislike in themselves. Intellectuals abhor "middle-class" norms because they are themselves imprisoned by them. The intensity of their critique of bourgeois society reveals the intensity of their implication in its problems.

Solving Social Problems

Homelessness and the underclass are social problems in the sense that they present a challenge to the entire society. But they are also social problems because they are exacerbated by broad social values, in this case an emphasis on external rewards. In general, the reliance on money, fame, and power as measures of personal worth result from the decline of other, traditional sources of purpose and meaning. Thus, intellectuals, more than any other social group, exalt external rewards because of their own extreme individuation. Lacking traditional, internal sources of self-validation, their only alternative source is external prizes.

The only escape from self-definition in terms of external rewards lies in rediscovering purpose and meaning beyond the self. This is a challenge that intellectuals face more intensely than others, because their individuation cuts them off more than others from traditional sources of meaning. Nevertheless, all Western people, particularly all Americans, must face this challenge—to reach beyond the self for values while retaining their cherished individual freedom.

The internal aspect of our social problems—the aspect slighted by emphasis on external rewards—makes it imperative that we focus on those people who in our society are both the most dependent on external rewards and the principal opinion makers: intellectuals. The trouble is that serious attention to this challenge can only be given by intellectuals themselves. Therefore, a real understanding of lingering social problems such as poverty and homelessness must await a willingness by intellectuals to look critically at themselves and their values. Until that happens, no possibility exists that these problems can be solved. In fact, until it happens, there is every reason to believe the problems will grow worse, no matter how rich society becomes or how many social programs the government enacts. External reforms cannot make everyone "above average"; they cannot mitigate what is essentially a problem of internal values.

This latter point speaks in an interesting way to Marx's famous remark that religion is the "opium of the people." Marx chides ordinary people for substituting something unreal and illusory (religion) for something real (social reform)—as if real reform could occur without the kind of spiritual transformation of each individual that it is the business of traditional religions to encourage. I would argue exactly the opposite: that genuine social reform is impossible without individual reform transcending the obsessions that most intensely afflict intellectuals and underlie their commitment to "social change."

7

The Dilemma of the "Authentic Black"

Many people take "underclass" to be a euphemism for blacks. The effect of this belief is felt in two quite different ways. On the one hand, the underclass is often regarded as a "black problem"—and by implication as not a significant problem for other groups. It is also widely felt that all blacks are in some fundamental sense disadvantaged, an entire segment of the population that society has an obligation to help.

It should be obvious to anyone who has seen the homeless in major cities that the underclass is not composed only of blacks, and therefore is not merely a "black problem." We can largely dismiss the first impression, then. Instead this chapter will focus on the other assumption: that idealism requires that we treat all blacks as disadvantaged, requiring our help.

The terms of the racial policy debate, as reformulated in the late 1960s, continue to drive our active policies today, especially affirmative action and busing. Moreover, the same assumptions govern much of the current discussion of other civil rights issues, notably those concerning women and gays. Thus the problem of group equality continues to be one of our major political preoccupations.

In looking at the situation of blacks, we must also come to grips

with the prevailing concept of the "disadvantaged" or "excluded"—
they used to be called "underdogs" or "outs"—who are the primary
objects of the left's commitment to equality. If one examines the
complicated array of people and groups who qualify and have
qualified as disadvantaged in our political debate, it becomes clear
that the "disadvantage" they suffer is very different from our common understanding of the word. In this chapter, I will argue that,
given the way we actually use the word, treating all blacks as disadvantaged is almost certainly retarding the quest by blacks and other
minority groups for economic and social equality.

I will begin by exploring how the concept of disadvantage has
changed over time, from something relatively simple to something
much more complex—from being defined in entirely objective
terms to something defined increasingly by subjective qualities. This
change reveals an extraordinarily rich and complex intellectual
drama, through which the left acts out its ongoing struggle with the
larger issues of freedom and order.

The Moral Battlefield

The English philosopher K. R. Minogue has set the background for
understanding disadvantage in his discussion of what he calls "suffering situations." "The point of suffering situations," Minogue
writes in his 1963 book *The Liberal Mind,* "is that they convert
politics into a crudely conceived moral battlefield. On one side we
find oppressors, and on the other, a class of victims."[1] The moralistic
emphasis on the evil of oppression reveals that a central element in
many people's definition of disadvantage is a desire for retribution
and punishment.

The concept of the poor as victims oppressed by industrial
capitalism began early in the nineteenth century and continues even
to the present day. In the last chapter I noted how the welfare state
has extended an important series of protections to people in demon-
strable and extreme material need; and how the substantial reduction in the number of poor has pushed our conception of
disadvantage in new, more complicated directions. The practice of
applying the status of "disadvantaged" to people not suffering from
income deprivation began at the end of the 1950s and early 1960s,
when blacks began to be seen as disadvantaged regardless of

income, even when unencumbered by Jim Crow laws. Today, women are thought to be disadvantaged, even if they do not work and are supported by wealthy husbands. (Some feminists believe that women are disadvantaged *especially* if they are cared for by wealthy husbands.) Although homosexuals are financially much better off on average than straight people (in large part because they tend not to have children), they too are considered in important respects disadvantaged.

When the concept of disadvantage embraced women and gays, the concern for suffering focused on issues more complicated than mere material deprivation—"disadvantage" became less objective and more psychological, existential, and subjective. Questions of whom the government should protect have been further complicated by environmentalists' concern about the natural world: forests, endangered species, and the general environment. These last changes in particular have caused confusion, because policies designed to help economically disadvantaged people often conflict with those that protect nature. Saving trees (for instance) raises housing costs for the poor.

The most important point here is that both disadvantaged humans and threatened plant and animal species are seen as "victims," to use Minogue's term. The assumption that all blacks are victims carries with it enormous, unintended consequences for individual blacks and for the black community as a whole.

In this chapter I will focus on blacks because the historical legacy of slavery has made them the archetypal disadvantaged Americans. At the same time, it is clear that although many blacks are disadvantaged, not all are, at least in the conventional understanding of that word. Nevertheless, the assumption that all blacks are somehow disadvantaged has an effect on every black person. Understanding the basic touchstones of disadvantage will also provide the beginning of a much deeper understanding of the left's larger search for meaning and its struggles to reconcile freedom and order.

The Costs of Being "Disadvantaged"

I began to suspect that "disadvantaged" had come to mean something more than simply weak, handicapped, downtrodden, and powerless when I worked for the California State Office of Economic

Opportunity in the early 1970s. I had simply thought the disadvantaged were the poor and the deprived, and that the War on Poverty was supposed to facilitate (as the legislation put it) "maximum feasible participation" for them in all OEO programs.

Nevertheless, I found that many people who worked at OEO were sympathetic only to certain people among the disadvantaged—those who made angry demands of the larger society to solve the problems they faced. At the same time, OEO workers were indifferent and often even openly hostile toward the poor who sought to find positive, constructive solutions to their problems. Among the black people they encountered, for instance, many OEO bureaucrats expressed a sense of kinship with those they regarded as "authentic blacks"—those who voiced deep anger, blaming the larger society, especially the white middle class, for their plight. To be considered authentic, a black person had to insist that society was not only responsible for his problems, but also for finding solutions to them. Those who failed to do this—those who did not define themselves by a preoccupation with the injustice of the system and by hostility to whites—were suspect; they were considered *untrue to themselves* ("Uncle Toms" or, if they were Hispanic, "coconuts").

Many OEO poverty workers believed that such people were unworthy to receive public assistance. Expressions of contentment or claims of success by minorities or the poor were taken as evidence of false consciousness. In recent years, several books have been written by black and Hispanic authors, describing the confusion and great difficulty they met with at the time when they denied being "disadvantaged."[2] The OEO radicals believed that only if the poor were politicized would they recognize their exploited condition and move to demand social change.

The effect of OEO policies was to discourage disadvantaged blacks from helping themselves and, instead, to foster dependency among them: improvements were to be granted by the government, not to be achieved by people struggling to improve their own lives.

OEO failed because it held a conception of community that offered the disadvantaged little real sense of belonging and no positive vision of a future to work toward. The program came to an end with the close of the 1970s. To a large extent the effectiveness of an entire generation of black community leaders ended at the same time. The black community has been searching for new leaders ever since.

Although people in those days talked in ways that seem extreme by today's standards, their claims—that "society" is to blame for the problems suffered by some of its people and that there is nothing disadvantaged people can do to help themselves—continue to dominate all social policy today. I can illustrate this point and its effect on its intended beneficiaries by considering a related issue: policy concerning illegal drug use.

The Implications of Our Drug Policy

Current policy, backed by the weight of public opinion, defines the drug crisis in terms of a conflict between two very different issues: the problems of addicted individuals and those of communities stricken by widespread drug abuse.

Although addiction hits every economic and social group, it especially afflicts the inner cities, which are torn by drug-related street violence. The trade in drugs has increased inner-city school dropout rates (as students are attracted by the money to be made in drug trafficking), corrupted law-enforcement agencies through bribery, and—in general and most important—demoralized entire communities with the example of crime that pays so well, when living an honest, moral life seems to yield so little.

Yet both public opinion and policy treat individual addiction as a greater problem than these social effects. And policy makers have concentrated their energies on dealing with addiction by suppressing the supply of illegal drugs through criminal prosecutions. In the process, almost everyone ignores—and, I will argue, even denies—the much more troublesome issue of the psychological roots of demand: why large numbers of people in all social and economic classes seek to anesthetize themselves regularly from the experiences of ordinary life.

The decision to concentrate on forcibly suppressing drug use and addiction has been a disastrous failure. While law enforcement officials have seized ever-increasing amounts of illegal drugs in recent years, new supplies have come to market so quickly that the street prices have in many instances fallen by half.

Policy makers have shown almost no interest in learning from the most successful rehabilitation programs ever conceived—Alcoholics Anonymous (AA) and its companion, Narcotics

Anonymous (NA). These programs are successful, as anyone with experience of either can testify, because of their radical, quasi-religious emphasis on empowering individuals to assume responsibility for their own problems, thereby to overcome them. AA does not blame alcoholism on liquor stores. In fact, a major reason AA enjoys success is that it treats all attempts to blame third parties as ventures in denial.

The principles that have made AA so successful could hardly be more different than those underlying current drug policy—and, not incidentally, those underlying all other forms of social policy. While AA believes that individuals can accomplish extraordinary things when they take responsibility for their own lives—when they strive to be their "higher selves"—all government social policy is based on notions of people as objects, without significant resources to solve their own problems. The social-policy view, which grows out of nineteenth-century attempts to apply the principles of natural science to understanding human problems, denies traditional ethics and dismisses appeals to personal responsibility as "blaming the victim."

One must acknowledge the special difficulties facing an inner-city drug addict seeking to conquer his addiction. Part of the cultural problem he faces, however, results from the social-policy belief that endemic socioeconomic conditions make it impossible for individuals in the underclass to do anything to help themselves. On the other hand, if an inner-city addict is to have a chance, he must believe—as Jesse Jackson might put it—that he is "somebody." Thus, successful inner-city programs, such as the Haight Ashbury Free Clinics in San Francisco, encourage individual responsibility and often make referrals to AA or NA.

The single greatest criticism of current drug policy is not that it has failed to curb availability, although it has indeed so failed. A still greater indictment is the policy's implicit denial of personal responsibility for drug use and the consequent subversion of an environment in which serious rehabilitation might take place.

The AA/NA system describes individuals who blame third parties for an associate's addiction as having a "codependent" relationship with the addict—of unconsciously and covertly supporting the addiction. Yet current drug policy and its supporting rhetoric can be seen as classically codependent—blaming drug dealers for the drug crisis. Whether they come from individuals or from government officials, such signals militate against the assumption of personal responsibility that is crucial for rehabilitation. The strategy of vigorous criminal prosecution of suppliers is the epitome of the codependent spirit that cripples our national policy.

The drug crisis exposes deep problems in our political discourse, whose antiquated, mechanistic notions about human possibilities deny individual responsibility. These same attitudes dominate the other major concerns of social policy, including what remains of our policy on race.

Codependency and Modern Social Policy

The belief that economic and social progress for blacks depends primarily on overcoming racist attitudes is another codependent attitude—precisely analogous to blaming drug dealers for the drug crisis. Focusing on white racism demoralizes blacks for all too predictable reasons: because it encourages the belief among blacks that they are without the power to help themselves, as well as the belief that all power over black destiny resides with whites. This view is most insidious when it pushes its adherents to reject black achievement and progress—even to claim, as in the case of the more extreme "authentic black," that success or progress for blacks in mainstream American society is a kind of conceptual mistake. Refusal of the responsibility of blacks for their own future, which is implicit in the messages of the old-line civil rights groups, subverts the sense of accomplishment and gratification felt by the large and growing number of blacks who have succeeded.

This denial of the ability of blacks to improve their own lot takes many forms. The black sociologist Kenneth Clark exhibited the problem in a *New York Times Magazine* debate with Carl Gershman. The conclusion that blacks continue to be victimized by white racism, he wrote,

> must be reached concerning those blacks who have made it into the middle class by means of jobs in corporate America. Many of these new black managers and executives are assigned to such race-related, "created" areas as "community affairs" and "special markets." They are rarely found in line positions.[3]

Another powerful statement denying the possibility of black success comes from Derrick Bell, former professor at Harvard Law

School, who argues in a recent book that blacks are "immutable outsiders."[4]

Few black leaders offer effective counterweights to this claim. During the 1988 election campaign, Jesse Jackson invoked a spirit of self-reliance in blacks, and this was one of the things that made him such an appealing figure. Unfortunately, he was ambivalent about his commitment: sometimes he summoned blacks to seize their opportunity and empower themselves; at other times he focused on black victimhood, draining much of the hope he initially encouraged.

Although the existence of white racism cannot be denied, continuing preoccupation with it undermines the moral and intellectual resources blacks need to achieve real progress. More than any legal or social barrier white society could have erected, this outlook holds blacks back. It is in fact the racist ideology of inferiority and dependency internalized. Many blacks have come to believe what racist whites have always said: "You can't make it on your own; you'll always need someone to help you, to do things for you." Nowhere are the effects of the victim identity on blacks more brilliantly analyzed than by Shelby Steele in his book *The Content of Our Character* (1990).

The view of blacks and poor as victims tends to politicize all of life, making individuals from those groups who do their best to participate in mainstream society seem the "class enemies" of those preoccupied with alleged oppression and exploitation. This denigrates the pride and satisfaction that those who have overcome "disadvantage" take in their efforts and tells them that, despite their accomplishments, they are really failures.

Those who choose to deny the ability of blacks to help themselves recite disturbing statistics concerning the worsening problems of the black underclass, without noting the substantial progress of the black middle class. Viewed together, these two phenomena indicate growing class differences within the black community. Between 1967 and 1978, black males who had not finished high school and had less than six years of work experience saw their average income decline from 79 percent of the average income of white males to 69 percent; meanwhile the average income of college-educated blacks with more than six years of experience *increased* from 75 percent of the average income of white wage earners to 98 percent. By 1980, college-educated black couples were actually earning *more* than their white counterparts.[5] The growing income disparities within the black community present a troubling picture combining success and failure.

The myth of black dependency on whites, unless debunked, cannot avoid becoming self-fulfilling. The power to stereotype is the power to control. Blacks' self-conception as victims of oppression has largely been sustained by civil rights groups and the opinion-making institutions with an interest in preserving the status quo long after it described anything real.

All of this has been the result of describing all blacks as disadvantaged, which made sense during the early civil rights days but disregards much more complicated issues facing blacks today. Instead of allowing blacks to develop for themselves in the manner of other groups in society, the civil rights movement has become an end in itself, its leaders bent on symbolic, superficial changes, neglectful of the need of black people to assume responsibility for and control over their own lives.

The Costs of Being a "Victim"

Treating minority groups as deprived and marginal to the mainstream of society is especially debilitating for natural leaders of minority groups, who can be strong leaders and serve as role models only if they overcome their deprivation and "make it." By asserting that, as "disadvantaged," such leaders cannot make it—that they cannot succeed and still retain "authenticity"—current social-policy attitudes thus enfeeble the leadership classes of minority groups and greatly hamper the constructive role they might play in promoting economic and social progress.

Author Richard Rodriguez provides a textbook example of this problem from an Hispanic perspective in his remarkable book *Hunger of Memory,* recounting his early life and his education at a university committed to affirmative action.[6] Although Rodriguez came from a "disadvantaged" family, and although he originally spoke only Spanish at home, he eventually was admitted to the Ph.D. program in Renaissance literature at the University of California at Berkeley. Along the way, he struggled to overcome the extreme alienation he felt from the "gringo" world outside.

When affirmative action appeared in the early 1970s, Rodriguez was eagerly pursued by university administrators obliged to fill racial quotas. He accepted his status as a member of a minority, but he chafed at the implication that he was disadvantaged.

Rodriguez's disillusion grew, and along with it his shame in playing his assigned role. He observed the cynicism of university "idealists," who praised obligation to the disadvantaged but left them unprepared to succeed in society, exposed to humiliation in front of their better-prepared classmates. He avoided Hispanic activist groups, which demanded that he "represent his people" and, when he demurred, attacked him as a "coconut," who lived for white approval. Finally, when Rodriguez was overwhelmed with job offers he felt came to him only because of his race, he couldn't take it any longer. He left the university and became a writer.

Along the way, Rodriguez became alienated from his family, a situation that made him feel ashamed. It is a common dilemma, experienced by those before him who rose above their backgrounds. But because he was educated during the 1970s, and because he is from a minority group, Rodriguez bore a special burden. Unlike earlier immigrants and children of immigrants, who were *celebrated* for their achievement, Rodriguez was *attacked* for it. This special burden explains why Rodriguez's book expresses profound anguish at the treatment the governing "idealism" regularly administers to members of minority groups who follow a similar path.

If Rodriguez were white, his experience of alienation from his family would be so commonplace, so normal, that no one would find it remarkable. His intellectual and emotional journey—leaving the shelter of family and local community and seeking an individual sense of self, trusting "lonely reason"—follows exactly the course that educated "advantaged" youth take.

The mainstream intellectual culture, however, will not concede the normality of Rodriguez's experience because it sees him as having disadvantaged origins. In the age of affirmative action, the left's concept of disadvantage decrees that he *cannot* succeed on his own. For if one person is acknowledged to have overcome disadvantage by himself, then the whole concept of blaming "the system" for disadvantage is called into question. This conceptual requirement explains the lengths to which the order left regularly goes to deny individual exceptions to its analysis of the incapacitating effect of disadvantage on its victims.

Because recognition of his individual accomplishment is

refused, Rodriguez's right to escape his background is denied; he is begrudged his right to participate in the larger intellectual culture as an equal. The real effect of this is to deny him the right to be an individual, apart from his role as representative of a minority group. This is most evident in criticism—mild from the white left and savage from Hispanic activists encouraged by the white left—that Rodriguez will not reaffirm his traditional identity as Hispanic and play up his status as disadvantaged. To be true to himself, his critics assert, he must be an "authentic Hispanic."

For Rodriguez the problem is actually far worse than a mere failure to be accepted for himself. For in the end the liberal culture actually *condemns* Rodriguez's individual successes, as well as his journey away from family and background, as violations of his essential self. He survives, but only at the price of an immense alienation that suffuses every page of his writings, and is communicated in a haunting, staccato style.

> Once upon a time, I was a "socially disadvantaged" child. An enchantedly happy child. Mine was a childhood of intense family closeness. And extreme public alienation.
>
> Thirty years later I write this book as a middle-class American man. Assimilated.
>
> Dark-skinned. To be seen at a Belgravia dinner party. Or in New York. Exotic in a tuxedo. . . . "Have you ever thought of doing any high-fashion modeling? Take this card."

Rodriguez survives because his religion provides a sense of belonging and continuity for him. Although he discusses this at length, few reviewers of his writings mention it. Acknowledging his religiosity, unusual among intellectuals, would require accepting his individuality and abandoning the view of his life as valuable only as a stereotype.

In meditating on affirmative action, Rodriguez criticizes the program as unfair and not helpful to those who need help most. But his most troubling observations are those that imply the devastating emotional effects that affirmative action has on its *beneficiaries*. Although they may succeed in their own right, they are not recognized as successful, which strains the relation between their public roles and private selves. This disjunction, formed in response to the manner in which he was regarded by his peers, is what finally drove

Rodriguez from the academy. He thus escaped the worst consequence of affirmative action: its delegitimation of personal success.

Affirmative action was initiated to overcome racial prejudice, but
it has the effect of encouraging the belief that any successful black
or Hispanic is a beneficiary of special treatment until proven otherwise (a nearly impossible requirement). The stigma thus attached to
members of minority groups becomes a barrier to employment and
promotion that no amount of legislation can correct. In delegitimat-
ing personal success, affirmative action also weakens the value that
public success holds for reinforcing an individual's private sense of
identity and achievement. Many "disadvantaged" people find they
can overcome the self-doubt that often goes with preferential treatment only by achieving a higher standard of performance than
suffices for the nondisadvantaged. Hence the reports from university
campuses of talented minority-group students who strain beyond
reason to get perfect grades, lest anyone think they are affirmative
action students.

Searching for a New Group Policy

The thought that affirmative action can help blacks comes from
commitment to a "group approach" to racial policy—one that attempts to predetermine the proportion of race and gender representation in education and employment. Like the belief that we can
solve our drug crisis by calling out the troops and sealing off the
borders, this policy is codependent in its spirit. It cripples the ability
of individual blacks to feel confident in themselves as individuals.
Efforts to fix the odds in favor of blacks only enfeebles them—
conspires in sustaining their powerlessness.

Affirmative action does nothing to strengthen the ability of communities and groups to empower individuals, because it has no
conception of how groups—understood as more than mere collec-
tions of individuals—can empower their members. Minority groups
grow stronger only when they develop strong leaders who succeed
on their own. The question thus arises: is it possible to treat all
minority-group members, especially the potential leaders among
them, as disadvantaged without destroying both the individual
strength and group reputation that is crucial to strong leadership?
How can the correction of past collective injustices remain the

centerpiece of policy without stunting individual success and achievement, which alone might allow transcendence of that past injustice? If we insist on treating all blacks as disadvantaged, how can we avoid actively punishing blacks who succeed?

In their concern for disadvantaged minority groups, advocates of preferential treatment believe—correctly, in my view—that deprivation somehow infects everyone in the group, and that relieving group deprivation is the key to correcting social pathologies. They also believe, however, that the distributive equality they claim we need is worth the price we would have to pay to achieve it. But the idealism is motivated more by guilty feelings about past injustices than by concern for future results; the desire for expiation distorts their assessment of how minority-group progress is best achieved. Preoccupation with past injustices blinds them to the truth that minority-group members can work for their own economic and social advancement. Countless success stories show they can.

Preferential treatment makes its mistake in interpreting a problem by focusing on group averages. Instead, we should emphasize empowerment of individuals, of whom the most important, in their influence on the group, are promising leaders. A focus on fostering self-reliance and self-improvement would encourage the emergence of a new kind of minority-group leader—an individual with strong local support, able to work independently of governments to build self-governing institutions committed to community self-improvement. Governments can support such efforts, but only if their help encourages independence and self-reliance—as so often in the past it has not.

The new generation of black leaders must reflect the diversity of the maturing black community. Moreover, the black leaders of the future must be concerned not only with countering disadvantage, as were the civil rights leaders of the 1960s; they must also provide leadership in the business of living, working, raising families, and building citizens and communities.

There are important indications that, ever since the mid-1970s, blacks have been assuming, on their own merits, a much more prominent presence in mainstream society than was possible amid the extreme polarization of the 1960s and 1970s. One can see it in films, in which blacks now routinely play nonstereotypical roles: businessmen, professionals, scientists, and spies. One can also see the beginnings of it in public life—the appointment of the first black national security adviser and chairman of the Joint Chiefs of Staff and appointments of blacks to lower-level policy positions in national security, economics, the environment, and many other areas. This trend is also indicated by the election of blacks as governor of Virginia and mayors of major cities that do not have black popular majorities, such as New York.

Developing strong minority-group leaders depends on understanding that the worth of leaders derives from their virtues and accomplishments as individuals—derives, in fact, from the sense that they have overcome obstacles and have succeeded—not from the prominence of their public roles. Affirmative action can grant a public position, but only at the price of demeaning individual achievement.[8]

Rethinking Group Equality

Underlying the belief that we can solve the race issue by preferential treatment is the idea that we can end inequality by ignoring differences in people's abilities and talents. This idea shows itself in "politically correct" terminology: for example, description of the handicapped as "differently abled," which in effect denies their disability. The implicit refusal to accept people as they are—as they see themselves—amounts to an insult so blatant that it throws many handicapped people into a rage. Feelings against such condescension are so intense among the handicapped that the quadriplegic cartoonist John Callahan has become a cult figure for fighting back through humor: by parodying the handicapped in a syndicated newspaper cartoon series that is one of the fastest growing in the country.[7] Callahan's cartoons stimulate incredible rage in return, but almost entirely from people who suffer no handicap. That people can regain their humanity only by subjecting themselves to ridicule highlights the perverse extreme to which we have been carried by our preoccupation with equalizing opportunity for external rewards.

If we cannot solve social problems by granting preferential status to the disadvantaged, where can we look for a solution?

Rethinking the issue of group equality will lead back to the conclusions we reached in the previous chapter about individuals. The possibility of equality for groups, like that of equality for individuals, depends on the emphasis a society places on the importance of individual or group achievement, measured in terms of some external value system. The more important success and achievement are taken to be, the greater the perceived inequality there must be, both for individuals and for groups. The stronger the emphasis on external standards of success, the more difficult it is to have a meaningful social pluralism, one in which real social tolerance becomes possible.

The greatest impediment to solving the problem of group equality is thus our intense and ambivalent preoccupation with external rewards. As I have already mentioned, this preoccupation is most strongly felt by intellectuals, who control our opinion-making institutions and thus our perceptions of all of these issues. Understanding intellectuals' attitude toward the disadvantaged in relation to this obsession—this ambivalent support both for external rewards and for cultures perceived to be antithetical to external rewards—may heighten appreciation of the depths of the problem we face.

I believe that the environmentalist movement has the most complex view of these issues—a vision far more sophisticated than anything in the objectified, mechanistic view of the old left. This more sophisticated view may offer a solution not only to the problems of the environment, but also, by analogy, to all our lingering social problems.

8

Environmental Schizophrenia

To judge from the vocabulary of the political debate alone, it might seem that environmental issues are understood only in negative terms, as "suffering situations" of an ecological sort. As such, discussions of these issues are attended by demands for punishment of polluters and similar wrongdoers. And environmentalists operating within the tradition of the politics of protest have, since Rachel Carson wrote *Silent Spring,* remonstrated against industrial civilization for ravaging the environment.

At a deeper level, however, environmentalists are searching for a larger, positive vision, one that transcends traditional adversarial politics. It is to be hoped that this search may light the way to a more positive, cooperative conception of politics in general. For it is in confronting issues of the environment that the intellectual left's search for new sources of authority and values—its attempt to integrate freedom and order—takes its most explicit form.

Trying to make sense of the debate on environmental issues is made difficult by the fact that two very different ways of looking at them compete for our attention. I distinguish these visions of the environment by using the words "sacred" and "mundane." The mundane view, consonant with the modernist spirit of the past three or four centuries of Western history, embraces man's right to subdue nature. This view, which takes it as "natural" for human beings to use the environment to suit their own purposes, has long underlain the modernist commitment to reason and science. Although the mundane view might seem inherently opposed to environmentalism, its desire to use nature implies the wish to use it both in the present and in the future; therefore, the mundane view uses both economics and science as guides for resource allocation over time.

The sacred view holds that man is responsible for serving nature. This position is akin to an older credo that stressed man's responsibility to things beyond himself, and it, or at least its spirit, now dominates environmentalist thinking. Although the environmental policy debate seems to be circumscribed by the mundane vision and its economic and scientific arguments, most environmentalists are, at heart, followers of the sacred view. They conceal this, however, because the sacred vision is so ambitious, challenging the governing assumptions of much of Western thought.

The heated quality of most arguments about the environment comes from the conflict between mundane and sacred views of the problem. Most conservatives, following their superior function in freedom, look at the environment in mundane terms; liberals, emphasizing order and including most environmentalists, usually hold to a sacred conception. Most conservatives rely on the economist's and scientist's tools of cost-benefit analysis to analyze environmental problems, while liberals often focus on much deeper issues involving man's basic self-conception as it relates to nature.

In important respects each view contains much wisdom. The tragedy in the contemporary debate on the environment comes when the two views are commingled. When that happens, as it does all too often, incoherence overwhelms all argument and it becomes difficult to support either position. The most prominent recent environmentalist manifesto that intermingles both views without clearly differentiating them is Vice President Al Gore's book, *Earth in the Balance*.[1]

In differentiating these ideas, two very separate environmentalist movements will become evident. Since each, in its way, speaks an important truth, no discussion of environmentalism can be complete without taking both ideas and movements into account.

The Mundane View

Mundane environmentalism is basically political, scientific, and economic, and its approach to environmental problems is primarily negative. The mundane movement treats environmental problems as instances of what economists call "market failure," and it is negative in that it focuses on stopping people from doing things—or at least raising the price of doing them (in order to discourage the behavior).

Market failure results from the underpricing of activities which in turn encourages a socially undesirable amount of them. With regard to the environment, examples of conditions leading to market failure include the lack of firm property rights to air and water, and the underpricing of publicly owned resources.

The absence of property rights produces external, or unpriced effects ("externalities," in the economic jargon), in which parties that use or abuse a resource impose costs on other users without paying for any harm that results. A classic example is air pollution: when an individual or business burns waste, causing pollution, neighbors lack an enforceable right to be compensated for their suffering. If polluting is, as in this example, "free" for the polluter, he may do it with abandon. This produces the economic problem of pollution, which is evident in controversies over the proper treatment of air, water, endangered species, and other resources with no clearly designated owner.

The underpricing of publicly owned resources produces another variant of market failure. This second type may be best illustrated by rush-hour traffic congestion. Since the government does not require drivers to pay the marginal cost of driving on freeways at rush hour, too much driving occurs then; but the only response our political leaders consider is to build more freeways. This same problem occurs in controversies over deforestation and acid rain as they affect publicly owned forests, toxic waste disposal on public land, the distribution of water in the western United States, and grazing rights on public land.[2]

One major and growing part of the environmentalist movement is devoted to finding economic, or mundane, solutions to these problems. The trouble with calling this approach "mundane" is that the word often carries the connotation of "unimportant." However, many problems that can be solved in mundane ways are very important indeed; they include even such enormous potential concerns as the "greenhouse effect," with its threatened heating of the earth's atmosphere.

Mundane remedies are not only those suited to low-level dangers; rather they are techniques whose use implies philosophical acceptance of man's right to exploit nature. Such acceptance is necessarily assumed in all attempts to measure "optimal" exploitation of resources by means of economics and science.

In trying to solve problems using mundane methods, environmental groups often work in cooperation with business. This has been especially true as environmentalists have become more sophisticated in their understanding of how distorted property rights create circumstances propitious for the worsening of environmental problems. The Environmental Defense Fund and other groups like it thus employ full-time economists to advise them on how such market distortions encourage environmental problems, and on how to fashion market-based solutions. By addressing the underlying distortions in pricing, such remedies can solve environmental problems systematically, by using the self-interest of private parties to accomplish their ends. The alternative is direct regulation, which must often cope with large-scale opposition and subversion.

Although the public debate has long assumed that the interests of business and environmentalists must conflict, there is no such conflict in the mundane vision. Businesses follow price signals, and if policy makers use price signals to accomplish their ends, businesses will cooperate. The business community has no reason to oppose legislative responses to market failure, provided the responses apply equally to all competitors. The recent history of environmentalist-business cooperation in addressing problems of strip mining, regulation of the chemical industry, and other issues confirms this point.

It is a pity that many environmentalists do not realize how effective economic analysis can be in solving environmental problems—in establishing the conditions for sustainable development. By arguing that we must somehow choose between economic and environmental values, they conspire to encourage development that is uneconomic *and* unsustainable. The Bush administration was unwittingly responsible for promoting the same error, by continually emphasizing the trade-off between jobs and the environment, as if those were the only choices. All of economics involves trade-offs; and when, for instance, governments underprice (and thus encourage overexploitation of) rights to cut down trees—as they do in most countries—their unsustainable policies must be understood as antigrowth, and they will cost future jobs when the trees run out.[3] The overriding issue is always: What is sustainable?

I must note here that not all instances of market failure are amenable to rectification by government intervention. In many cases, the high costs of solution exceed the potential benefits. When this is true, the mundane view of the environment counsels that it is better to do nothing.

Environmental Concerns as Issues of Ultimate Value

The mundane understanding of environmental problems exists alongside another, very different way of looking at them. This second view, which I have called sacred, embraces a far more ambitious project than the first: to change man's relation to nature, encouraging him to serve, not exploit, it. The sacred view is so different from the mundane that many people who embrace it feel they must automatically oppose the mundane view, just as they oppose business exploitation of the environment. Their desire to change man's relation to nature pushes them to oppose any effort (whether from business or environmentalists) that legitimates and thus encourages nature's exploitation.

Unlike the mundane approach, which is *negative* (telling people what they cannot do), the sacred conception focuses on the search for a *positive* way of relating to and serving nature. While the mundane movement receives its inspiration from modern, individualistic ideas, the sacred movement follows a much older, preindividualistic tradition emphasizing community and obligations. The sacred view is thus less political than visionary. Although environmentalists can seek to force us to serve nature by pushing for strict laws limiting our behavior, their ultimate purpose is to change our *internal* relation to nature, which of course no political action can accomplish.

The sacred view raises the ultimate questions of man's existence, especially his relationship with nature, the world, and the cosmos. Environmental theoreticians such as the late Aldo Leopold express this view by deploring the treatment of land as a commodity, which leads to its abuse. They argue, instead, for seeing land as if it were a community that we should love and respect. This sacred view appeals not only to concepts of ecology, but also to ethics. John Muir also wrote in this spirit as a diarist recording his experiences hiking through the Sierra Nevada, with every syllable radiating his reverence for the wild.

These two approaches to the environment—the mundane and the sacred—embody the two great ideas that are the subject of this book. They embody the polarities that we seek to integrate. The mundane idea, with its modern, individualistic underpinning, is aligned with the search for freedom; the sacred, emphasizing obligation and duty to something beyond the self, is connected with the yearning for order, virtue, and community.

The adoption on a mass scale of the more profound, sacred view occurred in the 1960s, when the New Left diverged from the old on a whole series of issues, but especially on man's relationship to nature. It is interesting that the same year, 1962, saw the publication of both the Port Huron Statement and *Silent Spring*.

The rise of the New Left caused great confusion among observers of Western politics, and the confusion quickly grew into hostility among many on the traditional left. By the early 1970s, when conflict over the Vietnam War was in decline, differing conceptions of the environment kept the New Left and old at odds. To understand more about these views and how they came into conflict, it is useful to recall the left's historical embrace of the ideal of progress.

From the Old Left to the New

Since the Enlightenment in the eighteenth century, the traditional left has been committed to the principal philosophical ideas of modernity: individualism, reason, progress. For roughly a century and a half preceding the mid-1960s, economic planning was a major vehicle of that rationalist belief. Throughout that period, "progress" meant material advance, economic growth, and—following the decline of traditional religion and its replacement by science's promises of secular redemption—the triumph of man over nature.

Until recently, social and economic planners were notable for their optimism. In the 1940s, when the idea of planning was at its apogee, there was hardly a problem or vexation of modern society that was thought to be beyond its ability to solve. Unemployment, slums, housing shortages—all were assumed to exist because of the inefficiency, haphazardness, or avarice of the marketplace. Planners thought that all these problems could be solved by transferring the powers exercised by markets to enlightened governments, in particular by vesting those powers in organizations of experts who would rationally survey society's needs and allocate resources accordingly.

In their optimistic pursuit of material progress, planners of the old left followed a path well traveled by the intellectual forebears of Marx. Marx himself was very clear in his belief that material progress is essential to the attainment of communism. Socialist theoreticians from the middle of the nineteenth century proceeded from a belief in a model society that would resemble a machine—a machine that could be designed, engineered, and controlled. Like Marx, they concluded that the inevitable success of the planning idea called for rebuilding the existing social machine—that is, the malfunctioning institutions of capitalism. The planners were going to redesign and fine-tune until they got everything right.

In the early 1960s the New Left began to question traditional commitments to material progress and economic growth. But although the New Left was hostile to planning in some important ways, it also laid the basis for a new form of planning. Instead of economic growth, the new planning would seek an end to growth. In place of the old optimism, a new pessimism spoke of a world of scarcity; it warned that we must conserve our limited resources and stop wasting them. Even the rhetorical case in support of planning changed abruptly: instead of attacking capitalism's failures, the new planning idea assaulted capitalism for its successes—for producing an abundance of useless consumer goods, imposing them on the public through advertising, and thereby despoiling the "quality of life."

It is easy to forget how abrupt and extreme was the New Left's philosophical disavowal of the ideas of their progressive predecessors—how it broke up all the old philosophical furniture. It attacked the old left with a vengeance and embraced ideas that seemed surprisingly "traditional." Where the old left had emphasized individualism, the New Left stressed community, adopting as bibles books such as conservative Robert Nisbet's *The Quest for Community*.[4] Where the traditional left had exalted individual reason and its instrument, science, while disdaining religion, the new reformers expressed great suspicion about reason, rejected science, and began a conspicuous search for new sources of religion and values, especially in the Orient.

Progress was the very heart of the traditional left's purpose, and science was its principal instrument, pushing forward man's historical quest to dominate nature. In the new vision, however, material progress was suspect, and the new planning for limits, exemplified in the environmentalist movement, was committed to the idea that man should accommodate himself to and harmonize with nature, not try to subdue it. The New Left even balked at the traditional left's reliance on the state and on political centralization as the principal institutional mechanisms of progress. The New Left was suspicious of all concentrations of power and authority, both public and private; and its rediscovery of community, especially small communities, conflicted in interesting ways with Marx's famous remark about the "idiocy" of village life.

The old left and the new do have qualities in common. The most important is that despite its apparent rejection of centralization, the New Left showed that it was very ready to call upon centralized power in pursuit of ends deemed to be of surpassing importance. Nevertheless, the intellectual perspectives of the two lefts are categorically different. Writing in 1937, George Orwell described a vision of socialist paradise that seems light years away from anything the new environmentalist planners have in mind:

> Socialism, as usually presented, is bound up with the idea of mechanical progress, not merely as a necessary development but as an end in itself, almost as a kind of religion. . . . The kind of person who most readily accepts Socialism . . . [also views] mechanical progress, *as such,* with enthusiasm. . . . As a rule the most persuasive argument they can think of is to tell you that the present mechanization of the world is as nothing to what we shall see when Socialism is established. Where there is one aeroplane now, in those days there will be fifty! All the work that is now done by hand will then be done by machinery; everything that is now made of leather, wood or stone will be made of rubber, glass, or steel; there will be no disorder, no loose ends, no wildernesses, no wild animals, no weeds, no disease, no poverty, no pain—and so on and so forth. The Socialist world is to be above all things an *ordered* world, an *efficient* world.[5]

Orwell, himself a socialist, abhorred this vision, but it was not seriously challenged among the mass of socialists until the appearance of the New Left in the early 1960s.

From the moment of its inception, the New Left set off in an entirely different direction. The Port Huron Statement sounds almost existentialist in its rejection of the old left's bureaucratic nostrums and in its embrace of "participatory democracy." Written largely by Tom Hayden, the statement was directed not at the left's traditional constituencies of the poor, blue-collar workers, and the disadvantaged, but at the young—students in particular—who rejected the very material affluence the old left had made its goal.

Although these differences were starkly prominent at the end of the 1960s, they are much less so today. Although the basic conflicts remain, in the early 1990s no one seems to notice. Liberal and leftist political candidates in both Europe and America regularly run on platforms promising more environmental protection *and* more aid for the poor, and the political culture sees no conflict. The philosophical differences that seemed to matter so much in 1969 now coexist, held together by a common opposition to the symbols of the traditional order—especially traditional religion and bourgeois democracy. In fact, although politicians have had trouble relating to sacred environmentalism, its complex understanding of whom and what our society has "disadvantaged" has brought about an important advance in the quest to integrate freedom and order.

Conflicts between the Mundane and the Sacred

There has been little disciplined debate on environmental issues because proponents almost randomly mix mundane and sacred arguments. And "opponents" (the quotation marks are necessary because I think most opposition is to the commingling of the two types of arguments, rather than to the substance of either) react heatedly to what seems incoherent. This incoherence was especially common and extreme in the early 1970s, when sacred positions were presented in apocalyptic terms. Thus, Lewis Mumford wrote in 1970:

> Nothing less than a profound reorientation of our vaunted technological "way of life" will save this planet from becoming a lifeless desert. . . . For its effective salvation mankind will need to undergo something like a spontaneous religious conversion: one that will replace the mechanical world picture with an organic world picture, and give to the human personality, as the highest known

manifestation of life, the precedence it now gives to its machines and computers.[6]

And Lee Loevinger, a member of the Federal Communications Commission, wrote in the same year: "Responsible scientific opinion holds that, unless present trends are not merely halted but reversed, there will be not more than 35 to 100 years to the end of all human life on earth."[7]

These statements are phrased as if they were supported by mundane (scientific and economic) analysis, but they are not. They make more sense if one thinks of them as sacred. As mundane statements, they would be subject to scientific analysis, by the standards of which they could neither be proved nor disproved using present-day knowledge. As sacred statements, they describe how many people felt, and still feel, subjectively, about the "disconnected" state of our relation to nature.

This is the cause of our environmental confusion: the use of mundane analysis to support the arguments of people committed to a sacred vision of the environment. Since the great majority of intellectuals are by temperament inclined toward the sacred view, incomplete analysis—even analysis unsupported by normal scientific methods—is often embraced by key opinion makers, especially in the media.[8] Calls are then heard for government regulations to impose billions of dollars of costs on alleged environmental offenders. All too often, however, we read several years later that the problem was not as bad as once thought, or that it was different in nature; often it becomes clear that money has been largely wasted. The most extreme case of this was the federal government's asbestos removal program, which some estimates projected would cost $156 billion. The program is now on hold, pending further study.

Many scientists, including those associated with groups such as the American Council on Science and Health, believe that the way to avoid such misuses of science is by stricter peer review—encouraging experts to stand up and insist on strict observance of scientific standards of proof. While there is merit in this suggestion, it misses a fundamental point. It fails to understand the impossibility of trying to use mundane arguments and analysis to rebut sacred arguments, since these two modes of understanding are drawn from different epistemologies.

Sacred environmentalists struggle with a great dilemma in

•

promulgating their message. Since their vision goes beyond an objective, external relationship with nature to a subjective, internal one, sacred environmentalists face enormous impediments to communication. Our public discourse has no place or categories for discussing internal concepts, and we do not have a language with which to discuss them. This only heightens the anguish and sense of urgency to communicate their vision that sacred environmentalists feel. I believe it is that heightened sense of urgency that underlies the apocalyptic tone of so much of our debate on the environment and that also explains the punitive cast of many environmentalist policy proposals.

Mundane arguments are also often doomed because people holding the mundane view usually cannot generate the passionate intensity available to those animated by the sacred. It is an uneven contest—not even close. It is not that mundane scientific and economic arguments do not win debates; the problem is that sacred environmentalists use mundane arguments metaphorically to press their point—just as people of the left at another time pointed to one Marxist regime after another, looking for a symbol of hope.

For this reason, mundane activists, such as Edith Efron and the late biochemist William Havender, are fundamentally misdirected when they criticize scientists who fail to oppose the misuse of science in support of the claims of sacred environmentalism. Those scientists understand the quixotic nature of the crusade to which they are summoned.

Nuclear Power and Radon

For most of the 1970s and 1980s, the debate over nuclear power was perhaps the most visible instance in which environmentalists warned about the dangers that science poses to nature. After the 1986 explosion of a reactor at Chernobyl in the USSR, popular opposition to nuclear power intensified, and the industry appeared to have no future as a feasible commercial venture in the United States. This happened despite the support of the overwhelming majority of experts on nuclear issues, who continue to regard nuclear power as safe and believe we should proceed with its development.[9]

Now the tide of popular opinion seems to be turning. Concern about the greenhouse effect is inclining some environmentalists, for mundane reasons, to look again at nuclear power, which is nonpolluting of the atmosphere. After all, educated assessments of risks associated with it were never very great. The best scientific estimates indicate that a large nuclear power program might reduce average life expectancies by one to one and a half hours, compared to dependence on coal-burning energy production, which would reduce life expectancies by ten to fifty days. The added risks from such a program would be comparable to an overweight person's increasing his weight by 1/100 of an ounce, or a highway driver's increasing his speed from 55 to 55.006 miles per hour.[10]

In contrast to the alarm caused by nuclear power stands the unconcern with the indoor air pollution produced by a radioactive gas called radon. Although naturally occurring, this gas is not naturally found in dangerous concentrations. But radon builds up indoors when there is insufficient circulation of clean air. Right now this pollutant is thought by some to be causing twenty thousand or more deaths per year, and to be the primary cause of lung cancer among nonsmokers.

The principal hindrance to air circulation in buildings is insulation, which Congress in the 1970s, using tax incentives, encouraged the public to install, in an effort to save energy. A little-known General Accounting Office report delivered to Congress in September 1980 contains some interesting information on the subject:

> The Department of Energy's recently proposed program to achieve more energy efficient buildings contains recommended actions to lower the air exchange rate, thus reducing energy usage. These actions (weather stripping, caulking, etc.) will allow less air to enter or leave the building, causing indoor pollution to substantially increase. [The Environmental Protection Agency] has taken exception to this aspect of the proposed program, stating that if implemented for all residences, the increased likelihood of exposure to radon alone could result in a potential increase of between 10,000 to 20,000 additional deaths per year due to lung cancer. DOE disagrees with EPA's estimate, believing the potential effect to be substantially less *because not every home will undergo the suggested buttoning up. . . .*[11]

The political reason why concern over nuclear power has been disproportionately larger than that over radon is that nuclear power is a symbol of our industrial civilization—and of our commitment to dominate nature. Exposure to dense concentrations of radon, in contrast, is a predictable consequence of attempts to reduce dependence on that civilization (by insulating homes, which reduces demand for industrial production of energy). In the realm of the mundane, radon is the far greater problem; in the realm of the sacred—which would have man alter his relationship to nature and the world—nuclear power is the cause of greater concern. This is because nuclear power is the outstanding symbol of the rationalist utilitarianism that sacred environmentalists seek to change.

The same kind of analysis explains why we worry about asbestos so much less rationally than we do about the burns from which asbestos provides protection.[12] It explains why we pay so much attention to the carcinogenic properties of man-made pesticides, but almost none to our far greater ingestion of carcinogens that are natural components of our food supply—*ten thousand times* as great, according to Berkeley biochemist Bruce N. Ames.[13] For the same reasons, the Environmental Protection Agency has directed all of its efforts to ensure food safety against relatively trivial health hazards such as the additive EDB, which Ames notes is a thousand times less potent a carcinogen in rats than the naturally occurring aflatoxin allowed to remain in peanut butter. Or, to cite perhaps the most notable food scare: Alar on apples, whose carcinogenic content is equivalent to that of one-third of a glass of city tap water. (No one has yet claimed that tap water is carcinogenic.)

An indication of the power of environmentalists' sacred view could be gained by asking if it would matter to them if alfalfa sprouts turned out to be as carcinogenic as, say, a synthetic food additive such as Saccharin. It would not. As many have acknowledged to me privately, they wouldn't care. Mundane information is irrelevant to deciding a sacred issue.

Sacred environmentalists, although not always rational, are not usually hypocritical. The sacred core of their vision belies efforts to discredit their motives. The most common of these efforts employs an economic, quasi-Marxist analysis to accuse environmentalists of self-interested posturing. Jokes such as "an environmentalist is somebody with a vacation home who wants to stop anyone else from building one" express this mistaken view.[14]

Although many policies designed to improve the "quality of life" do primarily benefit affluent environmentalists, mere self-interest does not account for the much more important *idea* that underlies this extremely important philosophical movement. For instance, although people with seaside views have a special reason for opposing offshore oil drilling, many people who have no such view and who live nowhere near the coast—and who have, perhaps, little interest in going there—oppose drilling every bit as passionately. For them, the *idea* is decisive.

Besides, no amount of greed for either wealth or power would begin to generate the moral fervor shown by environmentalists. Such fervor is the stuff of extreme idealism, or what I have been calling the sacred.

Growing concern about the environment reveals a deepening attention to issues of spirit, a tendency to move beyond preoccupation with external, objective phenomena as the sole arena of man's concern. Although concern with the external has dominated Western intellectual thought since the end of the Middle Ages, it was only a matter of time before man's advancing consciousness of self would force him to turn his attention inward once again. Sacred environmentalism has moved us far away from any objective definition of our problems and denied us objective answers. Now we find ourselves almost entirely in the realm of the subjective and of the spirit, forced to confront the question of how modern man, with his advanced consciousness of self, should relate to the world, to other people, and finally to himself. Although, until recently, political thinking seems to have ranked the importance of an individual's relationships in that order—first with the world, then with others, then with the self—the new imperative of self-governance almost certainly requires the reverse sequence.

In searching for ways to reconcile freedom and order, we must pay special attention to the sacred environmentalists' essential message. When sacred environmentalists push to change man's relationship to nature, they are trying, most fundamentally, to reduce, if not eliminate, the distinction between the ends we seek and the means by which we seek them. They are trying to encourage people to see all dimensions of life—even the normally deemphasized parts of it (the means by which they live, traditionally)—as valuable. In the most ideal terms, they seek to encourage people to see the means of life as, in effect, ends in themselves. Everything, in their view, is precious; nothing is valueless or without implications.

Put another way, the sacred environmentalists' challenge to man to "serve nature" makes sense only in the context of a society composed of people of advanced subjective consciousness, who no longer have the luxury of living mostly by habit. This implies, finally, going beyond the negative conceptions of truth bequeathed us by natural science. It demands that we seek positive conceptions that address man's dilemma as a being who views the world subjectively.

This environmentalist challenge has implications for issues that go far beyond the environment. It is also important for developing a new, subjective concept of disadvantage and the disadvantaged— for realizing a meaningful equality among people and even the rest of the world's creatures. Without such an understanding, no real respect among people and beings of different qualities, different endowments, is possible. Certainly no social policy bent on trying to achieve some crude material equality can accomplish this, even if material equality were achievable. What is the value of equal rewards if people don't treat each other fraternally? The qualities of spirit emphasized by the sacred environmentalists are indispensable to the realization of any meaningful equality, because only such a spirit can lead us to see the world as a community.

I might note here that the same basic issues are also evident in the debate over world peace. Both conservatives and liberals— "hawks" and "doves"—have until recently based their arguments on exclusively negative conceptions of peace. Neither side has had a positive vision. Hawks argue that the preservation of peace depends on military deterrence, while doves maintain that it depends on discarding weapons. The end of the Cold War seems to confirm the hawks' argument that the Soviet Union and communist countries were the principal threat to peace.* But confirmation of the hawks' "mundane" position on peace does not even address, let alone refute, the much deeper concern of many doves to find an *affirmative* vision of peace—to rediscover what it means to be peaceful. Such a vision is the analogue to environmentalists' sacred idea of a transformed relation between man and nature.

The emerging emphasis on spirit—on internalized values—is

---

*The period after the appearance of Soviet *glasnost* was the closest one ever gets to a controlled experiment in international affairs. One side (hawks) had argued that the communist bloc was the principal threat to peace. The other side (doves) said we were. One said they had to change; the other said we had to. When peace broke out following *glasnost*, it was hard to avoid the conclusion that the communists had, after all, been the problem.

also essential to working toward an integration of freedom and order. Reducing the emphasis on the achievement of ends, focusing on means as equivalent to ends, as having equivalent value, redeems the mission to live consciously that is the primary goal of intellectuals. Living consciously, attending to the implications of the means of one's life, also eliminates one's exploitation of other people—using them as the means to an end.

9

The Conflict of Core and Marginal

At a personal level, no group in society struggles more with the challenge of freedom and order than intellectuals and artists. We tend to speak about their struggles negatively, in terms of alienation from tradition. But it is more accurate to make the point positively and say that self-consciousness animates their need for freedom. The same self-consciousness in turn forces them to go beyond tradition and search for a form of order that positively engages them both personally and politically. At various times in the recent past, intellectuals and artists have looked to achieve this in political causes such as socialism and environmentalism. Such causes, in their traditional forms, cannot satisfy them because our politics is essentially negative and cannot yield a positive vision that will integrate freedom and order.

Understanding the dilemma of freedom and order requires recognizing it primarily as a concern of intellectuals. Intellectuals' struggle for synthesis, however, influences society as a whole. This is true for two reasons: first, because they control the intellectual idiom; and second, because they are the most modern of people, and their qualities of spirit provide a window on the future for all of us. Their dilemmas anticipate the struggles of the increasing numbers of highly educated people who will sustain economic growth in our postindustrial, information-based economy.

It is not surprising that until now all important efforts to reconcile freedom and order have attempted to *balance* the two. Such endeavors have taken the form of intellectuals' unremitting protest against "tradition," be it the liberal capitalist tradition of freedom in the West, or the Marxist-Leninist order in the formerly communist world. Whether "tradition" refers to freedom or to order, therefore, liberal intellectuals oppose it in their search to recombine the two imperatives.

In the United States, intellectuals such as Robert Bellah and Amitai Etzioni are now devoting themselves to striking a proper balance between freedom and order—between individualism and community obligations. In evaluating their effort, it is important to understand that balance is not the same as synthesis. On the contrary, balance implies a zero-sum-game, in which no synthesis is considered possible. For reasons I will explore, such balancing will not and cannot work. What is sought by modern people is not only a negative freedom from traditional order, but a positive freedom to consciously participate in an order that gives structure and meaning to individual and political life.

To make the point more concrete, I will introduce the concepts of "core" and "marginal," representing order and freedom, respectively. The dialectical tension between the core and the marginal (both of which may describe both people and values) is growing in our intellectual and social life.

Defining Core and Marginal

Core represents tradition, the cultural and moral "center"—the Establishment. For marginal intellectuals of the left in the United States and Europe, core represents the dominant traditions in the Western democracies: industrial society, the bourgeois achievement ethic, and the traditional moral and religious values of the middle class.

If core is tradition, marginal signifies freedom—for the left, freedom from tradition—in other words, anything opposed to the core. The marginal disposition to be in opposition to the core is reflected in the impulse to protest that inspires most leftist positions. It also inspires many conservative attitudes, though in a different way.

If marginal means freedom from the core, also implicit in it is a silent envy of the core and a desire to discover a new form of order that is consistent with freedom. Implicit in the marginal outlook, therefore, is the longing to integrate freedom and order.

Core people are ordinary working people, blessed with a basic acceptance of life—of themselves, of the (usually bourgeois) values of their parents, of the values of their country. Core people are committed to the world described by William Manchester in *Goodbye Darkness*—a world that has been declining for a long time and that in many ways seemed to have been finally weakened with the advent of the 1960s. Core people are bewildered by what has happened to the traditional world, which was often, though not necessarily, the world they grew up in. They are bewildered by why things "aren't the way they used to be." Everywhere they look, they see moral dissolution. They have become skeptical, but they have not become cynical. For example, while the Vietnam War made them wary of sending American troops abroad, they were cautious not because they doubted the fundamental morality of American intentions. Their caution came, rather, from doubt that Americans still had the will to carry through and win. If you had consulted core people before we invaded Grenada, they would have opposed the action. But when the invasion succeeded, core people—the overwhelming (and yes, usually silent) majority—backed President Reagan by an enormous margin. That the vast majority of people supported President Bush's decision to invade Panama reflected the same sentiment.

Marginal people, who often question and doubt their parents' values, also question and doubt the values of their society and country. With regard to our involvement in Grenada, as in Central America, the marginal left expressed nothing but severe moral reservations about American intentions. Moreover, their feelings—reflected in the mass media, for instance—remained strong even after it became clear that the Reagan administration's claims about Soviet and Cuban involvement in Grenada and Nicaragua had been true.

The response of marginal people to the Gulf War was special because of the Bush administration's extraordinarily successful efforts to build and sustain an international coalition of forces committed to the use of force. Only the extreme left, therefore, opposed the war; and its obvious success from the outset buried the few peace demonstrations almost as quickly as they began.

Marginal people have always been disproportionately numerous among intellectuals and artists, alienated as these groups often are from the mainstream of society. Since the 1960s, however, it has become increasingly possible to find marginal people among college-educated workers in nonintellectual fields. This is the *Big Chill* generation that experienced the 1960s and still feels its pull. It is the heart of the Democrats' yuppie constituency—marginal in relation to the values of contemporary American society, but not at all in relation to society's hierarchy of power. On the contrary, many of these people occupy positions of high social standing and wield great influence—as television newscasters, writers, clergy, business-people, and professionals of all sorts. Many of them are liberal in their opinions about social issues but relatively conservative in their views on economic policy.

Marginal people "think too much," in my mother's formulation; they (we) don't accept things. They oppose the social core in their search for new values, *and yet they depend on the core to resist them.* Marginal people are thus reactionaries in the most fundamental sense: they define themselves in opposition to the core—and I would argue that they do so in the face of a deep desire to *be* core. Unfortunately, they know it is impossible. It is in the very nature of marginal people's search that they cannot become conventional. Thus, when the core changes, so do they.

When core people get what they want, they are satisfied; they relax their opposition. When society as a whole adopts marginal positions, truly marginal people become anxious, even violent. They will look for new ways to be in opposition, either by escalating their old positions or by moving to new issues. What marginal people want cannot be given to them in externally measured, objective terms. In fact, it cannot be given to them at all. This was particularly evident during the 1960s, when radical protesters on college and university campuses made "non-negotiable demands." If university administrators acceded to all of their demands, the radicals invariably escalated them. Perhaps the best example of this occurred in the spring of 1969 at Cornell, where black radicals, finding revolution too easy, actually took to wearing bandoliers on campus.

The adversarial impulse in marginal people—the desire to oppose traditional values—is at the same time part of their search for new sources of order, for purpose and meaning. The predictability of their opposition has the unavoidable effect of making their commitments on political and social matters appear merely instrumental, devoid of content. But this hugely oversimplifies and underestimates their motivation. Marginal people's opposition is in fact part of their dialectical search for a way to integrate freedom and order—their quest to answer ultimate questions about the purpose and meaning of life.

In their search, marginal people are more confident about what is false than what is true—hence their emphasis on opposition. This is true of marginal intellectuals both on the left and, often, on the right.

If a stance of opposition is unavoidable to marginal people, it follows that no marginal position can be understood as a separate, discrete thing; it must be viewed, and can be understood, *only* in relation to what it is opposing—to whatever conception of the core it is pushing against. This means that marginal intellectuals' ongoing search will find them sometimes opposing freedom and at other times order, always searching for synthesis.

Since core refers to the Establishment in any society, and since Establishments can and do change, the notion of the core must be subject to change too. It can mean different things in different societies at different times. With regard to nineteenth-century Europe it means bourgeois society and the church. In twentieth-century India it means the traditional Hindu caste system and society. For Russia before 1917 it connotes the monarchy and church. For the USSR more recently it signifies Marxism and the ruling Communist party elite. Thus Russian intellectuals in recent times have opposed Marxism and looked to the West, while many of their Western counterparts oppose Western societies and seek to find an "ism" that will answer their societies' problems. Before long, when Russian democrats are firmly in power and out of danger from coups plotted by the *ancien régime,* we can assume they will become the new Russian core.

The New Left in the 1960s provided an excellent example of how intellectuals push against changing concepts of tradition. The experience of the New Left is one among many that confutes attempts to understand the core as simply traditional (or conservative) institutions and values. The New Left that appeared in the early 1960s was organized by extraordinarily marginal people. Yet it embraced many traditionalist ideas and rejected rationalist modes of organization, material progress, and other ideas of the old left. The new radicals often sought to live in rural communes and professed to hate cities.

In fact, they hated all forms of centralized, rationalized authority. The comparison to the marginal, reformist opposition in the Eastern bloc countries is very strong. In both cases intellectuals opposed what might be regarded as (extremely flawed) ventures in modernist government.

Marginal people in both the United States and Europe today find themselves in opposition to traditional religious authority, the values of bourgeois society, and the middle-class achievement ethic. These antagonisms define the essential positions of the political and social left, and the great majority of intellectuals feel naturally drawn to them.

The political positions taken by marginal intellectuals imply a call for the evolution of established order toward greater freedom, and then through freedom toward a new form of order, consistent with (and redeemed through) freedom. Since every marginal position, then, is "incomplete" (being by definition only part of a dialectical process), marginal people will begin to oppose each of their positions if they become too commonly accepted (and therefore core).

For example, in the seventeenth and eighteenth centuries the Enlightenment represented a marginal commitment to individualism, reason, and progress; it opposed the traditional religious beliefs that had started to recede at the end of the Middle Ages. But the earliest expressions of this marginal reaction—by Descartes, for example—maintained a fundamentally religious perspective. Not until the nineteenth century would marginal philosophers such as Nietzsche proclaim the death of God and call it a blow for individualism. But even then the problem of what to live for remained— what to believe in, even if you did not call it God. Spiritual questions were not settled and, given their very nature, could never be settled. It was thus only a matter of time until rationalist individualism itself became core, and a new generation of marginal people (the New Left) would repudiate it.

But, again, this rejection was not complete. Part of the synthesis modern people seek must include reason and progress. So the ultimate effect of the New Left's opposition to reason was to add a new dimension to the older, exclusive reliance on the mind and objective thinking. What the New Left introduced ultimately resulted in the increasing tendency of the left in general to consider internal, psychological, subjective qualities when attempting to understand

and aid the socially disadvantaged. This evolution, which I have already discussed, marks significant progress by the intellectual left in its search to integrate freedom and order.

In searching for a synthesis, marginal people, with their highly individuated conception of self, begin by opposing traditional values that seem to offer no place for conscious, individual choices about the values that guide people's lives. But many of the most marginal people today have found their way back to traditional institutions and values—although not always to the same values they first rebelled against. The San Francisco Zen Center, for instance, is full of marginal people utterly alienated from the mainstream of American social and economic life. But although marginal, the Zen Center is also very traditional, since Zen requires commitment to an enormously ordered life. In fact, Zen is far more ordered than were the lives that many of its communicants previously rejected as too confining.

Symbols of Core and Marginal

The notion of psychological "process" is extremely important in identifying marginality—*how* people come to do what they do, and how they actually do it. Is a conservative intellectual who is also a Roman Catholic core or marginal? Or neither? Has he completed his personal search and moved beyond marginality and the need to oppose? The answer depends on how he came to his current position, and on the nature of his current commitment. Was he born to his faith, and did he accept it as an unconscious commitment? Or did he embrace it in part as an adversarial act, directed against the agnostic liberal intellectual Establishment? If he embraced it as a conscious commitment, he is marginal.

Static roles do not satisfy marginal people; the need for existential engagement—touching their highly conscious inner selves—is of critical importance to them. Marginal people who end up at the Zen Center are not born into that way of life; they agonize their way and finally choose Zen. The Roman Catholic intellectual, in opposing antireligious intellectuals, leads an active, engaged life; there is nothing static about it. On the other hand, the traditional world of duty, honor, and innocence—the world portrayed in classic movies from the 1930s and 1940s—is static and thus finally unsuited to the marginal counterculture audiences those movies attract today. This is true however much such audiences long for the simplicity and sense of purpose they see in those movies, and however much they long to be free of the torments of their marginality.

It is easy to see why marginality is disproportionately common among intellectuals. Intellectuality expresses marginal people's need to examine the claims of authority and to challenge received wisdom. Moreover, it is not surprising that marginal people tend to be attracted to the verbal professions, from which they control the intellectual idiom that provides our framework to consider the political issues of the day. Marginal people are also attracted to the arts, concerned as they are with expressing their individuality and defining it in reaction to tradition.

Core values are exclusive; they appeal to the center of society and exclude those who depart from it. White Anglo-Saxon Protestants represent the traditional ethnic core of America, and preservation of their core values has become the province of the political right.

Marginal values are claimed to be "inclusive," appealing to all those who depart from the core. In saying that marginality is inclusive, however, it is important to remember that extreme marginal politics (of the revolutionary or totalitarian varieties) is every bit as exclusive as that of the core.

Although core culture tends to define its values without reference to marginality, and marginal culture is defined in opposition to the core, over time both are components of the synthesis we all seek. For this reason, neither has a truly independent existence.

The symbols associated with the core and the marginal can vary, depending on what is being compared; what may be removed from one center may be close to another. For instance, "ethnic" white people are marginal in relation to WASPs, but core in relation to blacks and Hispanics. Similarly, Jews historically have symbolized marginality, but to Western observers of the Middle East they are core vis-à-vis Arabs, because they share Western civilization and culture.

In considering these and other examples of the core and the marginal, it is important to be sensitive to the role of language. For many marginal people, for instance, "religion" is today a core word, and hence calls forth visceral rejection. The same is true of "God." "Spiritual," on the other hand, is quite acceptable to most marginal people. The core words describe traditional senses of religion; the marginal words describe a more experiential phenomenon.

Core and marginal connote basic moral, social, and religious values, and also a vast constellation of symbols for these values. Marginal people have created a language of symbols to differentiate themselves from and maintain their opposition to core values in almost every avenue of life. Partly because core people tend to be oblivious to this language and have difficulty understanding it, marginal people use these symbols to influence and to some extent control our political and social lives. When one "decodes" the symbols, one discovers how they do it.

Core in the United States is everything associated with middle America, with the middle class, its values and way of life—including its achievement ethic. Three-piece suits and Sunday church are symbols of core. So are short hair, TV sitcoms, and Old Grand-Dad bourbon. So are getting a "good job" and being a "responsible" citizen, John Wayne and Ray Kroc, baseball and bowling. Coreness is meat and potatoes, Budweiser, and instant coffee. It is *USA Today* and the *Wall Street Journal,* American cars and Akron, Ohio.

Core also includes symbols associated with authority: the military, the police, the church. In some ways, America itself is the most important symbol of the core in many other countries—a symbol therefore reviled by many marginal people in Western Europe and the third world. But America was also looked to as a symbol of hope by marginal people living on the other side of the Iron Curtain, who had to cope with a very different core.

Marginal symbols may include anything uncharacteristic of the core. An example may illustrate the importance of these symbols to marginal people. When Republican George Deukmejian became governor of California in January 1983, he succeeded Jerry Brown, a hyper-marginal Democrat. The story goes that, when Deukmejian took over, mustaches were the "uniform" of marginality in Sacramento. For reasons unknown, however, a number of Deukmejian's staffers took to wearing mustaches. When mustaches became associated with the very core Deukmejian administration, they could no longer stand as a symbol of marginality. Many liberal Democratic mustaches thus disappeared overnight.

Core people never retreat from their personal habits simply because marginal people start aping them. Most core people do not even notice. Marginal people, however, cannot tolerate core people's adoption of the symbols of marginality, because imitation kills their adversarial shock value. So marginal people move on, innovate, escalate—do anything to maintain their distance.

The most interesting thing about these categories is how they change: normally, as the core embraces the marginal, it forces marginal people elsewhere. Sometimes such shifts can signal broad ideological change. This happened in the early 1970s, when the New Left's decade-long challenge to the major ideas of the old left captured mainstream liberal thought, especially by inculcating suspicions of science, mind, and progress. Before the 1970s, the values associated with rich people were very core, and so were the symbols of their life-styles: big American cars, fur coats, good whiskey. In the 1970s, the tastes of the rich became marginal: foreign cars, foreign wines, exotic foods. A taste for things foreign is today almost always marginal; a preference for domestic goods is almost always core. Buying food at specialty shops is a sign of marginality, as is shopping in general at small "exclusive" retailers that offer personal service and allow one to avoid such "common" places as the A&P or Sears.

The fact that expensive consumer goods have now become associated with marginal is consistent with the phenomenon of the increasingly marginal upper-middle-class intelligentsia, whose members are the principal consumers of these high-quality goods.

Some of this concern with the symbolism of consumer goods can be quite snobbish and mean-spirited. Important elements among the marginal elites, for instance, consider tract housing core, and condominiums at Vail marginal.

Sensitivity to these categories is so great that actions inappropriate to one's perceived coreness or marginality can provoke funny reactions. When I was in West Berlin at a scholarly conference in the early 1980s, a Berliner friend took me to his favorite *Bierstube* one afternoon. To my astonishment and his delight, he ordered "Budweiser," explaining that it was the name of his favorite European beer—no relation to the American beer of the same name. The following evening at dinner with other American conference participants, I said I knew just the beer to order for us all. When the word "Budweiser" came out of my mouth, expressions of dismay appeared around the table. I felt guilty taking delight at their discomfort, watching them try to accommodate themselves to my embarrassing boorishness. The problem was not that they would be deprived of experiencing fine European beer; their real concern was that I had embraced the very symbol of the American core in utterly marginal circumstances. Their horror was rooted in the supposition that I was unaware of the enormity of my transgression. When I explained, they expressed their relief by unbridled laughter. (I might mention that my companions were all neoconservatives.)

The fascinating thing about core and marginal and the ubiquity of things that symbolize them is that marginal people often maintain a pretense that such symbols either do not exist or are unimportant. After all, it is not as if we have only a vague feeling for the language of symbols. We—or at least marginal people—have a remarkably refined understanding of these symbols as they appear in all areas of life.

I realized how well the refinements of the symbolic code are understood when I read sections of this chapter to friends and asked for comments and other examples. Again, the ability to respond was in every case determined by my friends' marginality, not their ideology. Whether they were conservative or liberal made no difference whatever. If they were marginal they knew almost immediately and exactly what I was talking about, and often debated at length whether I had identified taxonomic properties accurately.

Core and marginal have important analogues in moral and religious life. In the United States, for reasons already suggested, the Judeo-Christian God is core; the Hindu deities are marginal. The notion of sin is core; the Buddhist concept of the *ma* is marginal. Occasionally, however, a single institution or individual may adopt moral positions that place it or him in both camps. The Catholic Church is the very symbol of the institutional religious core (although fundamentalist Protestantism is the chief bulwark of the core code of individual behavior), but the Catholics made a real bid to be marginal on nuclear arms and (until the recent Papal encyclical) the ethics of capitalism.

The key to distinguishing between the core and the marginal lies in the qualities of the people to whom these terms are applied. If it seems to the reader that a dedication to order signifies core, and a yen for disorder or freedom signifies marginal, I must caution that the distinction is more complex. There is in fact core order and marginal order. Order is only core when it is traditional and habitual—that is, not the result of conscious effort.

Order can be marginal, providing that its adherents dedicate themselves to it by conscious effort, as do the practitioners of Zen

Buddhism and Yoga. Marginal order can also be found in the enormous physical discipline many marginal people impose on themselves today: eating well, jogging, exercising regularly.

Marginal can definitely mean "ordered"; in fact that is precisely the ultimate object of the marginal: to find an order compatible with freedom and the experiential questioning of received wisdom.

Implications for Politics

The distinction between the core and the marginal explains many puzzles in our politics. Normally one might suppose that most marginal people, who are on the left politically, would be hostile to capitalism and receptive to socialism. But in fact, attitudes depend on the type of capitalism or socialism in question. Capitalism, when it takes the form of big business, is core; and the left is hostile to it. Small business is often marginal. In general, mass-produced goods are core; high-quality (especially handmade) goods are marginal. For this reason, the most marginal leftists will love a capitalist who makes or sells handmade goods or health foods; and many will feel the same way of someone who makes or sells expensive consumer goods. If capitalists are producing or selling marginal goods or services, they are considered marginal—it's as simple as that.

Among "capitalists," managers are core, which explains the heavy support Republican political candidates generally get from the higher echelons of big business. On the other hand, many entrepreneurs are marginal—thus the large number of prominent Democrats among Silicon Valley tycoons. General Motors is core; Apple Computer marginal.

Until Mikhail Gorbachev changed everyone's perceptions of the world, many conservatives thought that the marginal left was "soft on communism," if not actually sympathetic to it. But again, it depended on the type of communism being considered. To marginal people on the left, there were (and are) good communists and bad communists. One might distinguish between the two by observing that communists are marginal unless they are engaged in running governments—especially the old-line Eastern bloc governments—in which case they are core. Communist leaders who were once revolutionaries remain marginal long after they graduate to running governments. But the people who succeed them are always perceived as managers, bureaucrats, functionaries—all definitely core. The USSR, from the time of Khrushchev to the rise of Gorbachev, was the archetype of core communism.

Gorbachev exposed all old-line communist leaders as core, and Lech Walesa, Vaclav Havel, and other marginal figures arose to challenge them. Fidel Castro has fared very badly in this process, as he has passed from marginal to hyper-core in the eyes of many on the left. This was clear when a *New York Times* op-ed piece early in 1990 compared him to Romanian dictator Nicolae Ceausescu.

The importance of the core and the marginal extends very broadly in politics. Most third world countries friendly to the United States are perceived as core, almost regardless of their internal ideological politics. Most third world countries hostile to the United States are seen as marginal. Almost no regime in the world was as ideologically offensive to the marginal left as the Ayatollah Khomeini's theocracy in Iran; yet one at first read little criticism of him and his mullahs in the liberal-dominated media. Although being rabidly anti-American was not enough to grant his government the status of full-blown marginality, it was enough to prevent his designation as core.

Similarly, Argentina, although it was run in the early 1980s by a ruthless right-wing dictatorship (a symbol of the core), was seen as marginal in its fight against the British over the Falkland Islands.

The concepts of the core and the marginal are important as well in trying to understand intellectuals' attitudes toward authoritarian and even totalitarian regimes. They explain, for instance, differing attitudes toward dictatorships of the right (core) and of the left (marginal), even when in "reality," as far as it can be objectively measured, the repressiveness of the two is identical. Many intellectuals felt understandably implacable hostility toward Nazi Germany. But for long there was nothing like the same revulsion felt toward the Soviet Union, which killed several times as many people as did the Nazis. The reason for the difference is that things celebrated by Nazi Germany (the Aryan race, German nationalism) were seen as core, while Stalinist Russia's exaltation of the world proletariat was viewed as marginal.

If I seem to be stretching things to call both Nazis and traditional Americans core, my point is only that the culture of each points toward and symbolizes the traditional "heart" of society. The totalitarian extremity of national socialism in Germany pushed the Nazis to reject everything in the moderate traditions of Germany, including religion. But they did so by pointing to a traditionally ideal type of German, in contrast to the totalitarian left, which celebrates an ideal "outsider" (proletarian). Different attitudes toward the core and the marginal also explain the double standard intellectuals have used to analyze Pinochet's Chile and Sandinista Nicaragua.

Core and marginal are also useful in understanding many intellectuals' commitment to the disadvantaged. In left-wing politics, it is chiefly those women who support feminism, those gays who support the gay rights movement, and those blacks who are most vocal in their demands for civil rights who are seen as marginal and therefore "authentic." These types also contribute the representatives one sees most often on the evening news, speaking for their groups.

Definitions of what is core and what is marginal not only can change, as we have seen, but have changed radically over the past twenty years, reflecting social and political shifts. Once one understands how the symbols of the core and the marginal change, the question arises whether they can deliberately be changed or even manipulated. An interesting opportunity for such manipulation arose when President Nixon visited China. Communist China was the very symbol of marginality until Nixon went there. After his trip it could never again be the symbol it had been. It became at least semicore. While this redefinition may not have been an explicit purpose of the trip, there is little doubt that Nixon and his secretary of state, Henry Kissinger, were aware of this result.

Over the past quarter of a century, China has been given an extraordinary range of symbolic faces. The distorting effects of the core/marginal metaphors were never more invidious than at the end of the 1960s, during the Cultural Revolution. During this period of brutality and terror, streams of Western leftists visited China and returned with tales of how they had seen the glorious future of man. Nixon's visit in the early 1970s confused China's marginal status and dimmed its reputation among leftists, but after Mao's death in 1976, Deng Xiaoping came to power as a new marginal leader. The forces he unleashed then proceeded to turn on him, repeating what he had done to Mao, an age-old pattern; the marginal turned core and (at Tiananmen Square) came into conflict with the rising new marginal forces.

The essential difference between the core and the marginal in the West today is that between the core pursuit of "a happy life," and the marginal search for "meaning." What drives marginal people in their restless search is the tension they perceive between stasis and activity; between being and becoming, between that which is habitual and that which is intentional and conscious.

It is important to remember that this tension exists mainly in the *perceptions* of marginal people—and this explains why they cannot be core, why they are compelled to undertake a search for new sources of authority and order. If their perception is overstated and exaggerated, it does not matter. The world runs according to perceptions of reality, not reality itself; and few perceptions are as important as those of marginal people of their need to search for meaning away from the core—and beyond it.

Core, Marginal, and the Political Right

Thus far in the discussion, I have focused exclusively on the marginality of the intellectual left. Is the intellectual right also marginal? One would think that if it is, something in the analysis must be faulty, because many conservative intellectuals support symbols and qualities associated with the core: Ronald Reagan, American automobiles, and middle-class values generally.

But the analysis *does* apply to many intellectuals on the right, and for the same fundamental reason: because conservative intellectuals share the same basic psychological, existential, and philosophical needs as those on the left. I refer especially to the commitment to reason and the fundamental reliance on experience rather than tradition for knowledge. Core values fundamentally fail for marginal people, and this is true no less for the right than for the left. Therefore, when conservative or neoconservative intellectuals defend traditional religion, they often do so somewhat disingenuously. The key word in that sentence is "traditional." Marginal, intellectual people can defend core values only for core people, not for themselves. Irving Kristol's statement that he is a "nonobservant Orthodox Jew" is a perfect statement of a marginal person who supports core values, but cannot fully embrace them because they are traditional. Marginal people must go beyond tradition to experience in their search for meaning; and for this reason core values cannot, by virtue of their being core, appeal to intellectuals.

The reason why many intellectual conservatives may be called marginal is that they, no less than liberal intellectuals, seek integration of freedom and order. They, like their counterparts on the left, seek new forms of authority and value; and they conduct their search by exercising freedom—by living conscious lives and discounting authorities that depend on preconscious habit for their allegiance. That is why, even when they are writing about religion, conservative intellectuals such as William Barrett, Peter Berger, Michael Novak, and others do so in a strongly experiential way.

When thinking about the relation between the core and the marginal in relation to the intellectual right, we may simply reassign every designation. The core that the marginal left opposes includes the business community and middle-class values generally. For marginal conservatives, the truly oppressive core is the *liberal* Establishment. By this conservatives mean the *New York Times,* the *Washington Post,* CBS News, and the Harvard University faculty. For intellectuals of the right, these are the truly powerful institutions of society—far more powerful than the U.S. Chamber of Commerce or Wall Street (symbols of coreness for the left).

In personal behavior, I know conservative intellectuals who go out of their way to drive American cars—core to liberals, marginal to conservatives. One self-proclaimed "second-generation neoconservative" even reported to me that a number of her Washington colleagues have come out in favor of smoking to express their marginal opposition to the liberals' campaign against smoking. Until his death a couple of years ago, a conservative political scientist friend of mine at Berkeley wore an absurdly frumpy baseball cap. It was clear that he did it because baseball is a core game, and he sought out opportunities to stimulate incredulity among his liberal colleagues.

Although the adversarial nature of such behaviors can appear trivial and silly, they are anything but. What they hint at is the ongoing search among both conservative and liberal intellectuals to integrate freedom and order—a search that is far more important than any other issue in our politics.

Understanding how American politics is really conducted in metaphorical terms will explain why so many people believe that our politics is in crisis—that it does not speak to the major problems that face us. In reality, it addresses a far deeper problem—the dilemma of freedom and order—which we must reconcile if we are to have any chance of solving the more superficial problems that preoccupy our political debate.

When considering the challenge of integrating freedom and order, it is important to understand that the challenge is not the same for core people as it is for marginal people. For core people, the challenge is primarily political—to fashion institutions that allow and even encourage full economic and political participation in their societies. This is the challenge that confronts the great majority of people in advanced industrial societies, including most people in the middle class (except the highly educated and artists). This challenge even confronts most low-income earners and minority-group members who are "disadvantaged." This political challenge does not pose itself to the same degree for the rich, even those who are core, because they can afford to buy their way into, out of, or around political institutions that deny real participation.

Marginal people, especially the highly verbal classes, control political institutions both directly and through their control of the opinion-making institutions including the mass media and the universities. The examples I have given throughout this book show the extent to which the crisis of our politics results from growing tension between core and marginal people over fundamental political issues. While marginal people use centralized politics to control and manipulate the core and its institutions and values, core people seek to increase their personal control over their own lives.

The quest to integrate freedom and order presents challenges both in politics and in people's private lives. Because they are more concrete and immediate, political solutions may seem the more important. But they are not. In the long run, the personal, existential challenge to integrate freedom and order is much more fundamental. Whether we meet this challenge will determine the future of our liberal political institutions. The importance of the personal struggle is grounded in the fact that it forces marginal people to grapple with the most basic issues of purpose and meaning in life. Moreover, all economic, social, and psychological trends are pushing people to marginality. The highly educated people who will be needed to run postindustrial society will therefore struggle, as most intellectuals now struggle, with the dilemma of freedom and order. They will struggle especially with how to answer the ultimate questions of meaning through experience rather than tradition.

10

Rethinking Basic Issues

Before searching for answers to the crisis in our politics, it is important to understand how the dilemma of freedom and order has come to us through history. How did our civilization move from the soft, slippery epistemological ground of medieval religion and faith, over the harder, seemingly more certain terrain of the Enlightenment reason and science, to a new soft and slippery, subjective, post-rational era? How did we find ourselves worrying about our spiritual relation to nature—trying to "reconnect" with the objective world? How, in our politics, have we moved away from our concern for the disadvantaged, defined strictly in objective terms by their poverty, to an increasing concern for those disadvantaged chiefly in relation to broad social values (in the case of gays) or in their social role (in the case of women)? And why, just as reduced international responsibilities are allowing American society to turn its attention inward, is public dissatisfaction with and alienation from politics exploding?

It will help to answer these questions if we go back and rethink some basic issues.

Looking Back

It was one million years—or three million, depending on when you start counting—between the time man's ancestors first climbed down out of the trees and the time men climbed into a space ship headed for the moon. How do we account for what happened in between? Why did man move from being a food gatherer to being a hunter and user of tools, then to being a farmer and builder of cities? What drove the Sumerians first to establish the fundamentals of religion, law, art, and science? What has pushed us since to develop these innovations in countless different ways?

The history of civilization is one of the progressive assertion of human will, a process that culminated in the seventeenth and eighteenth centuries in the triumph of science, reason, and individual rights. As man developed and imposed himself, the "external" limits on his powers receded: first small-scale threats to survival, then physical privation (in much of the world), and finally God Himself.

What has been the driving force behind this incredible social change, which has occurred in a relatively short time?

The tale of material progress, wherein man emerged from the trees and headed for the stars, is particularly perplexing when compared with the parallel chronicle of the human suffering that has scarred every century. The question is often asked: Why, if we can go to the moon, can't we solve our human and social problems? In searching for answers, people across the political spectrum agonize to discover what "went wrong" in man's human or spiritual endeavors. Although a nostalgic yearning for the golden past is more explicitly associated with the right, it is characteristic even of the left, as when Marx wrote wistfully about the Middle Ages, and Rousseau lamented the passing of the noble savage. The modern left also looks to the past when it celebrates traditional and non-Western peoples as representing ideals from which we have fallen.

The unwillingness to accept our condition and the desire to restore an idealized past have important implications for the way we think about contemporary problems. They explain why, although the left and right seem to reach opposite conclusions, their arguments—at least their arguments for altering the *order* of our society—sound oddly similar: both idealize the past, and seek to restore it, secured by some collective ideal.*

Rousseau states the basic progressivist position in his famous line: "Man is born free, but everywhere he is in chains." That is, man is naturally good but has been corrupted by faulty institutions such as family, church, and class. Reform institutions, say Rousseau and people of the left, and man will be free again.

In comparing the shortcomings of the present with the idealized past, the right draws the opposite lesson. The conservative view is a variant of the doctrine of Original Sin: man's nature is basically flawed or evil, and he needs institutions such as family, church, and laws to control and discipline him. Ronald Reagan spoke from this conservative premise when he said—as he often did—that the decline of religion and the family underlies social problems ranging from drug addiction to poor educational achievement.

It is interesting that the intellectual debate in all Western countries is largely concerned with collective and institutional questions, rather than those bearing on individual lives. While liberals argue that the central state is the principal instrument of economic and social progress, the right focuses its energy against the state (seeking to "get government off people's backs"). I refer here to the "superior functions" of both groups, the tendency of conservatives to favor freedom and liberals to favor order. Both also couch their political arguments in emphatically negative ways—freedom conservatives mounting their cannons against the state, and order liberals calling upon the state to combat or control all people and forms of behavior associated with "privilege."

All of this shows that the left and right argue opposite positions from the same basic assumption: that *institutional* reform—change in the powers and actions of the central government—is necessary to correct all fundamental problems. Both are preoccupied with the central state: almost no one is concerned with building positive forms of individual and community self-governance. Why is there no debate on empowering individuals and small communities, both public and private, to solve economic and social problems? In Chapter 7, I looked at this question in relation to blacks and other

---

*These positions of left and right *had* to refer only to the order positions of each because only the order positions worry about the decline of values. The freedom positions on both sides do not worry much about values, except negatively as they obstruct freedom.

minority groups, but it deserves to be asked throughout our political system, in relation to all groups and classes.

In focusing on institutions, the left and right see only a negative role for freedom. They are only concerned about freedom *from* things. Yet integrating freedom and order depends on conceiving a positive conception of freedom—connecting symbiotically with an order that encourages the participation of individuals and small communities in political and social life. We must admit the possibility—contrary to the hoary attitudes of both left and right—that nothing has "gone wrong" in our culture, at least not in the sense of straying from a better past that should be revived.

A Dynamic View of Human Nature

Part of what leads people on both the left and right to be critical of individualism and freedom is their attempt to conceive human nature in terms of a single unchanging assumption: man is good, man is bad, man is an individual, man is a social creature. No matter which of these presumptions is adopted, when one starts this way—without a place for a natural advance of freedom—one has trouble accounting for change. One must answer the puzzle of why, if man is naturally X, he has strayed from X. So, one ends up with the question of what "went wrong." This dilemma explains the stances of both the order left and order right in contemporary politics—implicitly attacking freedom for having put us wrong.

To replace mistaken assumptions about the unchanging nature of man, we must look for a dynamic principle, animated by the impulse to freedom—a principle that touches on and acknowledges all dimensions of man's nature and avoids trying to reduce it to a single principle. The force behind our animating impulse to freedom is an idea that since Hegel's time has grown in importance in our commonplace view of the world. It is the notion of the *advancing consciousness of the subjective self.*

Hegel was the seminal figure encouraging us to see the evolution of consciousness of freedom in almost every domain of social, philosophical, and artistic life. In fact, it is possible that the evolution of consciousness has animated the entire histories of philosophy, religion, art, and social and political organization.

The origins of advancing consciousness are understood both by philosophy and by religion as the natural desire for knowledge. In all religious traditions, consciousness or "knowledge" first appears in a myth similar to the myth of The Fall in the Old Testament. Eve's decision to eat of the apple in the Garden of Eden makes it clear that it is in our nature to have to choose—to leave the Garden. It is hard to avoid the conclusion that her choice was inevitable, since her very humanity made her, like all human beings, a creature able, and hence doomed, to choose. Human consciousness—self-consciousness—makes inevitable the need and demand for choice.

Although the will to consciousness, as portrayed in the Bible, is in our nature, the advance of consciousness has very complicated consequences. It brings great benefits, such as economic growth, increasing life expectancies, and the mastery of space; it also presents great (and I think growing) problems.

Understanding how this has happened requires understanding how consciousness has changed over time.

The Advance of Subjective Consciousness

In his book *Sincerity and Authenticity,* Lionel Trilling considers how the idea of consciousness has evolved in literature over the past four hundred years.[1] Identity and self-definition began with the moment when individuals began to play a role in history. It was a moment when men first became aware of what the historian Georges Gusdorf called "internal space." Before that, Trilling writes, man could not visualize himself outside his normal role; he could not imagine that he would be interesting to other men just "for himself," outside that role. The prerequisite to the emergence of the individual is the development of an internal, subjective sense of the self, and the ability to differentiate the self as subject (viewed from within) and as object (viewed from without).

To understand the implications of the rise of subjective consciousness and the subsequent exclusion of it from Western ideas, we would do well to recall the powerful appearance of the new concept in painting, around 1300. Two paintings, hanging side by side in the Uffizi Gallery in Florence and painted little more than twenty years apart, explain a great deal about the origins of our dilemma of how to integrate freedom and order. Both paintings are of the Madonna and Child—one by Cimabue at the end of the

Middle Ages and the other by Giotto, which declares by its difference the dawn of the Renaissance.

The first (Figure 1), painted by Cimabue between 1280 and 1290, presents an ethereal world, the imaginary product of an undifferentiated consciousness. Here the artist views the Madonna and Child as not sharply distinguished from other parts of the picture. This "holistic" quality is defined by a flatness of perspective, reflecting Byzantine influences that are more like Asian than later Western art. It reflects the preindividualistic perspective that we now associate with Asian philosophy and religion.

The best examples of such a nonconscious or preconscious state in our lives today are provided by infants and small children: they have little or no consciousness of self in the sense that adults have it. Nevertheless, anyone who has been a parent recognizes the myriad ways in which, from the earliest days of life, the development of a child's consciousness manifests itself. Children at about the age of five, for instance, are utterly unself-conscious in front of a camera; then, a year or so later, they can be terribly self-conscious—incapable of presenting a natural facial expression.

Twenty-plus years after the painting of Cimabue's Madonna, Giotto, who may have been Cimabue's student, became what we may call the first Renaissance painter by virtue of his radical advances in portraying man "in the world." (See Figure 2.) Cimabue's holistic consciousness has disappeared, and in its place we have the Madonna and Child set in a highly differentiated, naturalistic perspective. Most important, Giotto's Madonna, painted circa 1310, is a modern person, aware of her *self*, conscious of her separateness. If holistic "connection" is the essential condition of Cimabue's Madonna, the essential condition of Giotto's Madonna is *separation,* a differentiated state—indicative of the artist's more modern consciousness. These two paintings tell a story about the awakening of the inner person—the discovery of the inner self, animated by advancing consciousness of man as subject.

Over the centuries that have elapsed since the dawn of the Renaissance, this advancing consciousness has eroded authority based on convention and habit and forced increasing numbers of people, especially in the individualistic West, to redeem their lives through subjective experience. This advancing consciousness of the self is the reality that underlines our determination to integrate freedom and order. If "connection" was natural for the preindividualistic person, the new, differentiated consciousness can achieve connection only by conscious effort.

It is clear enough why Western social scientists, pursuing their ambition to study human problems with the objective research techniques of natural science, tend to avoid studying problems of subjective. The "scientific," "objective" orientation of academic psychologists eliminates it as a legitimate subject for study. Yet it is the central problem of our time, the central problem underlying the search, especially of intellectuals and artists, for new sources of ꜰꜰꜰꜰꜰ ꜰꜰꜰ ꜰꜰꜰꜰꜰ

As I have noted, advanced individual consciousness provides great benefits—it permits innovation, resourcefulness, economic growth, and the sense of being "engaged," aware of living life to its fullest. In fact, these benefits are so many and so great that even if they could, most people would not give them up in order to "go back" to some imagined happier, preindividuated state.

But beyond the benefits it confers, the advance of subjective consciousness is also the cause of severe social strains. It is responsible for the enormous problems that socialists mistakenly attribute to capitalism—especially the deteriorating authority of cultural values and a growing sense of inequality that plagues societies that prize individual achievement. Such tensions almost certainly harm economic performance, as demands for government action to resolve them lead to policies that encourage economic inefficiencies and distortions.

Subjectivity and Separation

In modern times a great contradiction has come to plague Western thought. This contradiction is most obvious in the completely different epistemological assumptions that we take to be true in our public, as against our private, lives. It is also obvious in our embrace of reason, science, and objectivity as guides to our political lives even though subjectivity, transcending reason and objectivity, dominates our personal lives. This contradiction will become clearer as we recall the two great approaches to knowledge and truth that compete for our allegiance.

Since the time of the Enlightenment, intellectuals have been committed to reason and the scientific method as the only legitimate

Figure 1. Cimabue, *Madonna Enthroned,* from Sta. Trinità, Florence, c. 1280, Galleria degli Uffizi, Florence (photograph courtesy of Alinari/Art Resource, N.Y.)

Figure 2. Giotto, *The Virgin with Child and Angels,* from the Church
of the Ognissanti, Florence, c. 1310, Galleria degli Uffizi, Florence
(photograph courtesy of Alinari/Art Resource, N.Y.)

means of understanding scientific, and by extension, social scientific, reality. For at least three centuries, emphasis on the objective has been the centerpiece of intellectual thought, advancing knowledge beyond the superstitions and unverifiable claims associated with medieval religion.

The objective tradition rests on the belief that the only reality is external, independent of interpretation by the mind. Until fairly recently not only was it unfashionable to talk about subjectivity in relation to modern scientific questions, but Marxist and liberal political thinkers banished it from all discussions of political and social affairs.

Meanwhile, beginning in the eighteenth century, a very different way of approaching the arts and philosophy made its appearance. The new tradition, which emphasized subjectivity, burst into full flower at the end of the eighteenth century in the Romantic movement, notably in Goethe's Germany, and then was elaborated philosophically in the nineteenth-century existential writings of Kierkegaard and Nietzsche. Emphasis on the subjective has grown through much of our own century, and in the past thirty years especially, as writers, poets, and philosophers have celebrated the importance of subjective experience in individual and social life.

Subjectivity implied a liberating but sometimes unhappy acceptance of individual separation. The first existentialist, Kierkegaard, proposed a "leap of faith" to religion in an effort to find a bridge back to order. Nietzsche said this was hopeless, that God was dead. We were, he claimed, alone.

Are we alone? Is there truly no path to order or "connection"? The answer depends on whether a new meaning can be found for "subjectivity," one that can help us integrate freedom and order. Such a meaning would be quite different from the Romantic sense, and it is crucial that the reader understand the difference.

In the sense that it has been expressed through the arts since the eighteenth century, "subjectivity" emphasizes an inner emotional need to express individuality, often by rejecting traditional social values and roles. This kind of subjectivity has become a powerful force in our individual lives as well as our political and social life. It has had both positive and negative consequences, for example in its challenge to the confinement of conventional sexual roles, which has set off a process that generated the women's movement, legitimated divorce, and provoked demands for economic and social equality of the sexes—the right to be mothers *and* wage earners. Subjectivity in this sense has certainly been turned to positive effect in psychological counseling, which encourages people to discard burdensome social constraints in favor of values and relationships validated by personal experience. Nevertheless, on the negative side, subjectivity has also seemed to encourage widespread narcissism.

Subjectivity and Politics

The "Romantic" concept of subjectivity is reactive and tied to emotions. We fear the effects of this form of subjectivity on our politics. We sense that, cut loose from cultural norms and objective authority, people will be unanchored, bereft of the guidance and restraint that social life requires. We shrink before the Nietzschean nightmare, in which moral authority is dead and personal responsibility has no meaning, in which might makes right, and every impulse is given free reign.

Fear of subjectivity is especially acute for conservatives, who believe that Western society has survived only by virtue of its tenuous grip on the spiritual and moral anchor of traditional authority, especially traditional religion. Since Romantic subjectivity seems to be the intrinsic enemy of tradition, conservatives' fear of it is particularly pronounced.

There are in fact very good reasons for fearing this idea of the subjective. The 1960s revealed some of them, especially the danger of assuming that the marginal revolt against the core represented the completion of a search for values—that opposition represented discovery, that liberation from traditional authority was the same as realization of one's true self. Opposition, however, does *not* represent discovery. It is only the first (negative) step en route to the positive goal of self-actualization.

After the 1960s, as things calmed down, the emotional force of the great upheaval was spent. But the tendency to apotheosize marginal and radical leaders that was so powerful in the 1960s remains strong in our intellectual and social idiom. In the 1960s and into the early 1970s, many observers failed to see the harbingers of authoritarianism in the celebration of radical violence. This blindness was especially acute on university campuses. Once regarded as bastions of openness and tolerance, by 1968 the universities had become intolerant of ideas that departed from a new and narrow orthodoxy. They had become, in fact, our most conspicuous centers of the authoritarianism of ideas.

These problems continue even today, especially in the debates on environmentalism and feminism. They remain evident on university campuses, where the movement for "political correctness," with its elaborate rhetorical prescriptions about approved and nonapproved words and phrases, represents the most recent marginal attack on core values. As in the 1960s, little inclination is shown to oppose radical students' disruptions of speakers expressing presumably unpopular views—views that elsewhere might be regarded as moderate. This phenomenon points up a certain left-liberal indifference to authoritarianism when it comes from the left (that is, when it is marginal).

Marginal hostility to core positions is evident even in (supposedly) value-free social science. In a famous experiment conducted at Yale in the early 1970s, social scientist Stanley Milgram concluded that there is an intrinsic conflict between authority and morality. His "scientific" finding merely reinforced the long-standing myth, commonly held on the left, that authoritarianism is a perversion associated only with the societal core.[2] Although Milgram does not reach this conclusion, many people believe that authoritarianism cannot exist in "revolutionary" regimes, no matter how repressive.

The blindness of marginal intellectuals to revolutionary despotism comes ultimately from their need to find new sources of structure and authority. Their search has become frantic in modern times, as the traditional sources of structure and values—family, church, and local community—have declined. The tendency of marginal intellectuals has been to look to the state and the central government as the source of new authoritative values.

Burke's statement that society needs "a controlling power upon will and appetite" addresses part of this problem. Burke approached the issue from the standpoint of a defender of the traditional political and social order, whose vulnerability to authoritarianism results from the need of individuals for personal structure. When people can no longer find structure in family and church, they seek it in government, which is often only too happy to respond.

Government responses reach their greatest extremes in totalitarian regimes, which are sustained by ideological myths. The problem of totalitarianism—of an authority carried to its extreme—is an outgrowth, as psychologist Erik Erikson once put it, of the popular longing for *totalism*. This is the longing for a complete, pure myth to explain the world and man's place in it. The abuse of such a myth is symbolized easily and always by Nazi Aryanism. But Aryanism is an example of only one side of the totalitarian problem—the core myth, meant to appeal to the extremes of core values of society.

At the opposite pole of totalitarianism are marginal myths—the myths of "world brotherhood," of the "international proletariat," of Rousseau's General Will, of the "authentic black"—that are as hostile to individual freedom and self realization as the myths of the most ossified traditional systems. On the surface, liberation is the very essence of revolutionary idealism. Yet underneath, like the core myth, the marginal myth is oppressive. In practice, idealism born of reaction against core authority has often produced intolerance as great, and even greater, than that of any traditional authoritarian regime.

Revolutions prosecuted in the name of liberation, justice, and the remaking of a bankrupt society are guided by psychological intolerance—intolerance not of authority, but of its *breakdown*. Hence the apparent paradox that liberators often end up enslaving. What they seek liberation from is uncertainty.

Francis Fukuyama has written that the collapse of Marxism in the former Soviet Union and its client states has brought history to an end, and that liberal democracy will henceforth dominate the earth. It is stunning to read long critiques of Fukuyama's essay "The End of History?" that fail to point out that subtle shifts in ideas about liberal democracy may threaten to destroy it from within. For example, the shift from concern for the rights and well-being of individuals to concern for groups (ethnic, sexual) poses a great threat to our institutions. The threat will be especially great if leading opinion makers fail to see it.

Preparing for this peril and meeting its challenge depends on finding new sources of authority and values—new sources of order—that are consistent with individual freedom. In searching for these, the essential question is: What sort of order will people consciously accept; and under what conditions will they accept it? Increasing numbers of marginal people, especially among the highly educated, cannot find purpose and meaning in core institutions, which fail to provide them latitude to satisfy their gripping need to question and understand. It is not that some churches, for example, are not trying to change this. Movements for the ordination of women certainly represent such an attempt. Yet the churches undertaking the most liberal reforms continue to lose adherents, because their reforms are seen as superficial and piecemeal. Established religions continue to fail to touch the essential, interior dilemma of marginal people, who see their efforts at reform as no more than concessions to the secularism and objectification that are overwhelming modern society.

The crisis in our politics emerges out of core people's demands for control over their own lives—over the political and social institutions that most affect them—at a time when marginal people are trying to use centralized politics to conduct their search for a new order.

Core people desire freedom from constraints placed on them by government at the behest of marginal people. Marginal people are pulled by their own need for freedom within a framework of order; yet they have often sought it in a self-deluding embrace of structures and dogmas more oppressive than traditional authority in its darkest ages.

The problem of conflict and differences between core and marginal people inheres in the advance of modern subjectivity, and it will get worse. As the marginal search for a new order intensifies (strengthened by the continuing advance of consciousness), marginal people can be expected to intensify their reactive opposition to core values. Since marginal intellectuals use their control of our intellectual idiom and political institutions to pursue that opposition, our political crisis will worsen as the search for a new, marginal order leads to an ever more centralized political control of core culture.

As we look for solutions to the dilemma of how to satisfy both groups' demands for freedom and order, one of the principal shackles we must discard is the mechanistic, Newtonian worldview that continues to dominate social science (and therefore the political debate) long after it has been discarded by its mother-science, physics.

Integrating the Personal and the Political

There is one other reason why it is so important that we develop a post-Newtonian response to these issues, and that is to close the enormous gap that exists between the personal and the political, between reality discovered subjectively and objectively.

Our public life and discourse are focused on a world of objects—ideal, externally defined things—that bear very little on the private issues that affect our subjective experience. These private issues are important, for they provide the context in which we relate intimately to others and in which we understand personal meaning.

The standard of judgment we bring to bear on politics is very close to that of old-time religion, as our political debate is torn by heavy moral judgments that are of condemnation and abomination. When we judge elements of our private lives, we abandon this harsh standard. No one would think to use the word "evil" to describe one's child or relative. When we are personally close to those we observe, we use a modified, "therapeutic" vocabulary. For example, we might criticize the behavior of someone close to us by calling it "unhealthy," because we know that such a softened appeal to health is more apt to affect that person's behavior than is stern moral condemnation. In their private lives, most people find that positive reinforcement works better than punishment, especially with fellow adults and children as they get older (infants and small children are a different matter). We have no sense of how to employ these positive techniques in public debate, however. We know only how to threaten, denounce, and punish.

Most people believe the language they use in their private lives is more accurate in judgment and effective in persuasion than the language that dominates our politics. The two can become more alike only when we allow the concept of subjectivity to influence our political vocabulary. The ultimate reason we need a subjective means of discourse is to encourage observers of social and political life to take themselves and their subjective viewpoints into consideration when making observations. Traditional social science, like the natural science it imitates, has no concern for the subjective and pretends no capability to study it. Yet the basic dilemma of reconciling freedom and order is forced on us by the advance of subjective consciousness and the growing alienation of individuals trying to "reconnect" with the objective world around them. This reconnection is attempted by core and marginal people in different ways, politically and individually, but it remains a challenge to all of us, to change the way we think about different kinds of relationships—economic, political, and personal.

A New Concept of Subjectivity

Ironically, in moving beyond the world of objects and exploring subjectivity, we must commit ourselves to doing so *objectively*. Allowing subjectivity into intellectual and political discourse cannot mean throwing away all reason and objectivity. But because subjectivity so plainly influences our political, social, and psychological life, the failure to admit it into intellectual debate violates any meaningful standard of objectivity. Objectivity, after all, requires seeing all dimensions of reality on which there is wide agreement; and ignoring what is so manifestly important mocks our commitment to be objective. It is also true, however, that to discuss subjectivity rationally requires that we develop a new concept of the subjective—one that does not simply surrender to unreason.

To analyze subjectivity objectively, we must find an idea of the subjective that goes beyond the purely reactive notion conveyed by the Romantic tradition in the arts. Recognition of the importance of man's subjective consciousness is not merely an argument for allowing individuals *more* expression, *more* freedom, *more* democracy, *more* equality. Rather, the emphasis should be on subjectivity as meaning "from the perspective of man as subject"—accounting for man's consciousness of self. This implies a creative element of positive volition that is lacking from Romantic subjectivity, with its emphasis on emotional reaction. It implies that we *must acknowledge our need for individual expression in order that we may explore its effect on our related need for personalized order.* Only by seeing and accepting this reality can we find an objective foundation on which to build meaningful, purposeful, conscious lives. Continued denial of the importance of subjectivity only precludes fruitful discussion of the conditions that underlie the profound pessimism and sense of hopelessness that are so prevalent today.

The need to satisfy their subjectivity affects both core people and marginal people, pushing both toward a new concept of order, though in different ways. It leads core people to seek control of their economic and social lives through political self-governance. It pushes marginal people to seek the end of personal alienation that results from their internal feelings of separation from others and from self. What is needed is a vision of order powerful enough to attract the voluntary allegiance of core and marginal people alike. What intellectual discipline might we hope will help in the search?

Two disciplines stand out: psychology and physics. As the most basic science, physics has contributed abstractly—breaking down the separation between subject and object, insisting that observers of phenomena include themselves in what they observe.

Psychology was the first social science to move beyond a myopic focus on the objective. After World War II through the 1950s and into the 1960s, humanistic or "third-force" psychology explored the expansion of human possibilities through a cognizance of subjective consciousness. In the late 1960s this theoretical work became the foundation for the human potential movement, and the dawn of the New Age was upon us.

Although "serious" people ritually dismiss the importance of New Age thought, these ideas have had a far greater influence on our political, social, and economic life than most people realize or will admit. Although many people associate the New Age only with flaky spirituality, the fact remains that, in its essence, the New Age, the human potential movement, and their humanistic psychology forebears represent an effort of psychologists to go beyond the deterministic, "scientific" theories associated with behaviorism and Freud. Their essential purpose, as I understand it, is to find a subjectivity that is *creative,* conscious, and animated by will. In trying to rediscover a concept of individual will, which the older psychologies had worked overtime to exorcise, the humanists have helped revolutionize important areas of our social and economic life. This change may someday allow us to move beyond the reactive, exclusively emotional, Romantic subjectivity and regain an element of personal self-governance. Already, the humanists' rediscovery of will has touched everything from management theories (which call for increased participation of workers, less reliance on top-down command systems) to social relations (including less reliance on hierarchies and inflexible roles).

The great challenge we face today is to bring these same approaches, embodying participation and self-governance, to bear on our political system.

11

Political Crisis and the Centralized State

In the United States and practically everywhere else, the political crisis is the crisis of the modern, centralized state. Modern politics *is* the politics of the centralized state, and its dilemma is rooted in the long history of the centralized state's rise and decline.

In recent years many countries with strong, centralized governments, including especially many socialist countries, have stumbled badly because, although designed to serve the public welfare, their political systems ended up serving the private interests of the people running them. The essential problem is that centralized governments do not encourage or even allow meaningful participation by citizens in the institutions of their own societies. Most important, they do not allow *self-governance,* by which citizens govern their own lives through voluntary cooperation devoted to common purposes.

Renouncing the deceptive idealism that underlies the centralized state is difficult, in part because the rhetoric supporting it seems to appeal to man's better impulses. Consider the words spoken by New York Governor Mario Cuomo in his 1984 keynote speech to the Democratic national convention:

> We Democrats still have a dream. . . . We believe in a government strong enough to use the words "love" and "compassion" and

175

smart enough to convert our noblest aspirations into practical realities. . . .

We believe in a single fundamental idea that describes . . . what a proper government should be. The idea of family. Mutuality. The sharing of benefits and burdens for the good of all. Feeling one another's pain. Sharing one another's blessings. Reasonably, honestly, fairly—without respect to race or sex, or geography, or political affiliation.

We believe we must be the family of America, recognizing at the heart of the matter, we are bound to one another, that the problems of a retired teacher in Duluth are our problems. That the future of the child in Buffalo is our future. That the struggle of the disabled man in Boston to survive, and live decently is our struggle. . . . That the failure to provide what reasonably we might, to avoid pain, is our failure.[1]

The image of central governments as families could not be more appealing. It also could not be more impossible. The trouble is, central governments are *not* families. They lack the very qualities of proximity and affinity that make families able to do the things Governor Cuomo extols. Compassion and empathy, like trust, are qualities nurtured in personal, not impersonal, relationships. Families, neighborhoods, local communities—these intimate units perform the functions Governor Cuomo describes, because they are organized around personal relationships. Central governments are rational, abstract communities, which cannot replace intimate communities because they are centralized, physically distant, impersonal, and— despite any good intentions—uncaring.

This has been true of all central governments everywhere, throughout time. Central governments can establish broad institutions, laws, and policies—the ground rules that establish and maintain a productive order. This is their most important role. They can provide basic amenities for people in need, and they can protect individuals from abusive treatment by other citizens and authorities, up to a point. But when they preempt the role that only local institutions can play, that of provider of care and community, they drain all humanity out of political and social life.

That is just what is happening in our politics today.

The myth that central governments can "do it all" comes from our attempt to model political thinking on science, with its negative understanding of truth as the absence of falsehood. Like science, the myth of the all-powerful, beneficent government is also based on a negative vision—that of a political community devoted entirely to preserving individual rights, protecting citizens from harm or unfairness. But a government based on rights can never offer a positive experience of community. Its failures to do so take two different forms: for people in trouble, it cannot offer the nurturing, personal embrace of those close by in clan or neighborhood. Nor can it offer better-off citizens the positive sense of community that comes with self-governance and volunteerism.

Politics focused on the centralized state is the political and social analogue of Newtonian physics and its mechanistic assumptions about the universe. There can be no solution to our political crisis until we focus on building a post-Newtonian, nonmechanistic conception of *governance.* Governance, in this sense, is a multilayered system that permits individuals and communities to determine the rules that govern institutions close to them. By relying on reciprocal individual contributions that work to the common benefit, it emphasizes unity through respect for diversity and cooperation among individuals and groups.

In trying to reconstruct our local institutions, we must understand that the crisis of confidence in our public life extends to all major private institutions as well: corporations, labor unions, the medical profession, the legal profession, churches, schools.

I have noted that the decline of confidence in these and other entities has continued more or less uninterrupted since the mid-1960s, when surveys of public confidence in institutions first appeared. In their classic study of the subject, *The Confidence Gap,* Seymour Martin Lipset and William Schneider blame declining confidence on the adversarial stance assumed by television news.[2] When television became the principal provider of information about the world during the 1960s, it helped change the way people in the advanced democracies viewed themselves and related to institutions.

The Changing Terms of Identity

Growing consciousness of the personal, subjective self is radically changing how we define personal identity. Before modern times, identity was primarily a matter of place and status: people defined themselves as bricklayers or bankers, as members of particular families or local communities, as Catholics, Jews, or Protestants, as husbands or wives, and so on. However, more recently and since the 1960s in particular, identity based on status has been losing its attraction even for many core people. Increasingly, identity is defined not in relation to the static question, What is my place? but to dynamic questions: What do I think, feel, and do? How shall I live? All this reflects the influence of the subjective, pulling people to weigh values and relationships in terms of an internal, subjective standard.

The definition of personal identity now seems to be a *process*—a complex activity of determining values that provide individual purpose and meaning. But values provide meaning only when they are both understandable and understood. Values imposed by traditional authority, adequate for lives conducted by tradition, provide no sense of meaning for highly conscious, marginal people, and less and less meaning for core people as well. This is why my generation—obsessively self-conscious—"thinks too much." Younger generations are even more uncertain. And even our parents to some degree seem uncertain of things they knew with certainty in the past.

This changing view of identity is affecting the nature of personal relationships. In the past a sense of duty and obligation provided the social glue that connected people: husbands with wives, employees with supervisors, children with parents. In the 1950s, before the bonds of traditional relationships were fatally weakened, an established hierarchy held relationships together: fathers told their children what to do; wives were expected to support and be directed by their husbands; employers gave orders to employees. Before this time and for all of human history, social bonds were hierarchical, and convention set the terms of cooperation and relationship.

In the past three decades, however, as notions of individual freedom and "rights" have gained strength, increasing desire for personal expression has undermined these hierarchies. In this time, all types of relationships have undergone fundamental changes, and yesterday's "leaders"—fathers, husbands, bosses—have lost much of their authority. Cooperation among people has increasingly come to depend on *consent.*

This change in the basis of personal relationships has brought forth an entire literature of "how-to" books, teaching people how, under the new rules, to relate consensually to others. These books teach people how to love, how to manage, how to raise children; they teach people how to relate to each other not as objects, but as subjects. The enormous success of Thomas J. Peters and Robert H. Waterman's book *In Search of Excellence,* which concerns relations in the workplace, speaks precisely to this radical change in the nature of authority. In the same way, books with titles such as *Do I Have to Give Up Me to Be Loved by You?* tell people how to integrate the desire for connection (order) with the need for self-expression (freedom) in love relationships.

The reasons why the basis of relationships has changed so suddenly and profoundly are complex. Affluence   a radical diminution of physical adversity (including, I would say, the end of the Cold War and the decreased likelihood of large-scale international conflict)—is no doubt partly responsible. The media have contributed their influence, and there have been other factors.

Although such "explanations" are interesting, they are not, in the end, terribly important. Even if some people see the changed view of personal identity as a problem, no one can imagine any significant retreat from it. Moreover, whatever immediate causes seem important, the ultimate, underlying cause—growing consciousness of our subjective selves—reflects social and psychological trends that go back centuries.

The Changing Role of Institutions

Television played a special role in accelerating these changes during the 1960s when it brought to people a sense of immediate relation to events occurring outside their own families and neighborhoods. In the process, television substituted *communication and experience* for *custom,* sustained by habit, as the principal influences sustaining, or undermining, institutional loyalty. During the 1960s, television brought images of weakening institutional authority into every living room and thus hastened the process of its decline. More specifically, it conveyed the exuberant, even chaotic, self-expression of that time, multiplying people's sense of personal choice and challenging their allegiances.[3]

Throughout history, institutional loyalty had been maintained by custom, and in this crucial sense all institutions had been bastions of coreness. Then, in a very brief time every institution was forced to move from core to marginal—to rely for authority not on custom, but on efforts to *earn* allegiance.

The substitution of communications for custom means more than just revising the messages that institutions send to their followers. At a time when reliance on custom and traditional hierarchy has all but expired, earning allegiance also depends on the ability of institutions to listen to and *hear* their followers. It depends on radical decentralization of authority, allowing "followers" to have a greatly increased say in controlling their own lives.

The crisis of authority has developed because no institution— neither governments, corporations, churches, nor any of the others—has any experience in using communication in this way to sustain its authority and following. They have traditionally sought to reinforce custom and passive compliance through appeals to duty, patriotism, and piety. Increasingly, they must engage the active support of self-governing adherents.

Besides organized religion, two sectors that have responded least well are government and large corporations, which are among the most hierarchical and least participatory of institutions. The corporate failure to listen to consumers and employees is a major reason, I believe, why the Fortune 500 largest U.S. companies lost more than three million jobs during the 1980s, while the American economy as a whole was adding nearly twenty million new jobs. And continuing anger about their failure also explains (I believe) much of the recent flap about high corporate salaries.

Smaller, more entrepreneurial companies are less hierarchical, more participatory, and therefore more able to satisfy the desire of consumers and employees for self-expression and self-governance. Thus it was management guru Peters, I think, who said that any organization that has more than sixty people working for it is in trouble. Enterprises can be larger; but as they grow, the tendencies to hierarchy intensify and they have to work harder to maintain self-governance.

Initiatives to "privatize" or decentralize private organizations are sometimes referred to by the word "intrapreneurship." Gifford Pinchot III is the leading authority in the United States on intrapreneurship. Leon Louw and Frances Kendall have been very successful with their Free Market Foundation in South Africa, teaching corporations how to decentralize authority by spinning off functions that would be performed better by independent units.

But although the trend toward self-governance is affecting every sector of society, I want to focus on how this movement is manifesting itself in our political institutions, and what we can do about it.

The most interesting demands for political self-governance may be found in the efforts of low-income and minority-group communities all over the country to gain control over the institutions that most affect their lives. The spread of self-governing ideas is the most important recent development influencing opinion and policy as they relate to education, public housing, local community organizations, and social services.

Both political parties—Democrats and Republicans, including the conservatives and liberals within each—are conspirators in an effort to foil this movement. Both parties want to control governance, but not to have to work too hard to change society. Both would rather bask in applause for their self-proclaimed wisdom or compassion.

Democrats think everything happens in Washington: the only way to fix society's problems is to spend more money, to grease the big federal machine so that it works properly. They believe the poor and minority groups cannot really run their own lives. Although many of them would be loath to admit a commitment to bureaucratic management of the poor, that is where their policy prescriptions and political alliances tend to lead. They have shown little interest in working to stimulate low-income people to achieve real self-governance, because they are convinced that self-governance only benefits the well-to-do. For the disadvantaged, only the national government machine can provide.

Republicans are no better. While they talk a lot about getting government "off people's backs," most of them are content to see social policy administered from afar. They may believe in the ability of people to run their own lives—or at least say they do—but very few of them have shown any interest in actively working to empower low-income and minority groups at the local level, helping them to acquire the skills and financial help they need to make themselves genuinely independent. Most Republicans' interest in the machine of government is strictly negative: they want to stop it. George Bush's secretary of housing and urban development, Jack Kemp, is an exception. He wants to make the system work to empower people, and I will be surprised if he is not elected president someday for his efforts. If he is, he will be supported by a new political coalition incomprehensible to people who take present party allegiances as definitive.

Anyone who tries to understand the appeal of Ross Perot's sporadic run for the presidency in 1992 in simple left-right terms will understand nothing. Perot's populist appeal was to people all along the political spectrum who want to take back control of their lives.

This point is also hard for people working in the national media to understand. Especially if they happen to be based in one of the nation's power centers (Washington or New York), journalists embrace our centrally focused political system because it reflects its power and prestige on them. Their "Beltwaycentrism" blinds them to major changes that are transforming our politics and ideas of governance.

We would do well to contrast the downscaling of private business—its move to more entrepreneurial forms—with the unrelenting centralization of power and authority that continues in our politics. Some statistics will illustrate this. Since the founding of the republic, for example, Congress has passed 350 statutes preempting state and local authority. Half of these (180) have come in the past twenty years. The growth of federal regulations is indicated by the swelling size of the *Federal Register.* Its pages increased from 3,140 in 1937 (its first full year) to 20,174 in 1970, to 87,267 in 1980. Under President Reagan they declined, dropping to 53,822 in 1989, the first year of the Bush administration. They have since increased again, reaching 67,871 in 1991.

These numbers translate into the mountains of regulations that must be scaled by would-be entrepreneurs. The burden of this task falls more lightly on big businesses, for they possess the resources to avoid or deal with such regulations. Small and medium-sized companies, however, are often discouraged from forming, driven out of business, or forced to combine into larger enterprises capable of defending themselves.

One significant response to this increasing regulation is "informal" markets, through which citizens, consumers, and entrepreneurs take matters into their own hands. For example, instead of submitting to the dictates of building inspection departments entombed in red tape and wielding rules that systematically force people to overbuild their houses, citizens and the contractors they hire often ignore the regulators and complete home additions on their own. Similar behavior is occurring in many other areas of economic activity, which adds to the growing alienation of citizens from our political system. The fundamental problem is wholesale institutional failure.

Another adverse symptom of political centralization is the implicit shift from our system's historical concern for the rights of individuals to a new concern for the rights of groups. This new attitude is especially obvious on university campuses. Both admissions and faculty hiring are increasingly influenced by racial and gender quotas, which, although not officially endorsed, are in practice almost everywhere.[4]

The transparency of the pretense that selection by quotas is not practiced is yet one more reason for popular disillusionment. In the end, such policies can only turn group against group, and people against people. They have inflamed racism on campuses. And when university authorities enforce bans against speech considered denigrating to certain groups, the result is an ever greater feeling of strangulation by artifice and hypocrisy. All of this, I must repeat, is a consequence of our growing preoccupation with external rewards to redeem identity.

Emphasizing Self-Governance

Our political culture—and again I refer to that engaged in by both political parties—is overwhelmingly in complicity with these practices. Nevertheless, a few individuals stand out in trying to forge a new path. They are changing the world by combining the left's compassion for the downtrodden with the right's belief in the ability of people to help themselves. Besides Jack Kemp, these include Leon Louw and Frances Kendall in South Africa, Hernando de Soto in Peru, Muhammad Yunus in Bangladesh, the late Mohamed Salahdine in Morocco, Mimi Silbert in San Francisco, Sy Fliegel in East Harlem, Polly Williams in Wisconsin, Robert Woodson in Washington, D.C.—and the numbers of such people are growing. When they reach a point of critical mass, our social and political landscape will change forever.

The question they pose is not whether government should be replaced by no-government; it is how publicly funded services should be delivered. The key distinction is between government's *providing* public services and its *delivering* them. At present, public services tend both to be provided (funded) *and* delivered (performed) by governments. From schools to housing to legal services, public services are "delivered" by an all-powerful government to people who have no say in shaping the services—no part in deciding what they get or who gives it to them.

Viewing public services as something merely "given to" people implies a one-way transaction—delivery from the top down. Never discussed is the single element crucial to the success of all such services—namely, recipients' involvement in their implementation. To believe that problems can be remedied simply by giving things (e.g., federal money) to people is Newtonian fantasy.

Self-governance stresses governmental responsibility for provision and local control of delivery. It implies participation from the bottom up by recipients of assistance.

Unfortunately, our present-day public discussion of these policies tends to be conducted in a spirit not very different from that with which we discuss the feeding and care of farm animals. The focus is all on ends, with almost no interest in means.

People are not farm animals. In the implementation of all social service policies, the participation and self-governance of recipients makes the difference between success and failure. Participation will determine whether schoolchildren learn, whether the unemployed acquire new job skills, and whether recipients of all forms of rehabilitation assistance (criminals, drug addicts, alcoholics) overcome the behavior that got them in trouble.

Participation is important for reasons beyond these narrow, utilitarian purposes. Active participation by citizens, working to achieve the collective economic and social purposes of a society, is a necessary element of a healthy democracy. Participation and self-governance are good in and of themselves apart from any benefits they yield in achieving social ends. They are important as *ideals,* because they are essential parts of society's encouragement of individuals to live full, realized lives.

It is easy to see why the public has withdrawn from participation in most arenas of "public life": because it has been left no room to do anything except passively receive things from what many state and local officials refer to as the "national delivery system." People know that government has made a mockery of the original notion of "public" policy, and they want no part of it.

It does not have to be this way. Governments can provide

services without also delivering them. They can pay and leave delivery up to others, as they did after World War II with the GI Bill. At that time, the U.S. government wanted to provide access to higher education for returning war veterans but did not want to create and run a lot of colleges for them. Instead, it provided vouchers (the equivalent of money), which were redeemable at accredited colleges. Choice of institution remained with the veterans.

This bill, which allowed millions of young people a chance to go to college, is the model for a very different way of organizing public services from any we have at present. Structuring our political system to encourage real participation and self-governance by citizens would end the crisis in our politics by restoring to people control of their own lives.

The importance of participation highlights the importance of *choice.* The search for self-governance must begin by acknowledging this crucial element, which empowers people to have a say in all parts of their lives. This is especially true in regard to social services. The principle of choice implies the right, within limits, to choose the provider of a service—whether it is a school or a lawyer or a drug addiction rehabilitation program—and it also ensures the recipient's influence on the nature of the service and how it is given.

Recognition of the right to choice is based on belief in the self-governing capacities of the overwhelming majority of human beings. It is based on the understanding that without opportunities for choice and influence, the hope of real commitment of or involvement by the recipients of services is retarded, if not extinguished. Meaningful participation is impossible without the right to reject one form of participation (for example, in a particular school or program) for another. The rich take this right for granted: they hire their own lawyers, send their kids to the schools of their choice, and, if necessary, select their own rehab programs.

In fact a radical shift toward the provision of subsidies to individuals rather than service providers has begun to occur. In education, this is evident as a large and growing movement has appeared to push for choice in education, for allowing parents a role in selecting their schools. More than twenty states are today considering allowing some sort of choice system in education; several major cities, including New York and San Francisco, have made commitments to implement choice systems in their schools; and blacks and other minority groups are strongly represented among supporters of the movement.[5] Subsidies for housing are increasingly given as vouchers to tenants rather than as grants to failed public housing authorities.

Following are some possible applications of the principle of choice to social policy.

Education and Choice

In times past, government-supported schools were truly "public," because they were run in close consultation with representatives of the local communities they served. Today, especially in big cities, such schools are run by huge bureaucracies; kids are often bused far from their own neighborhoods, and the schools are no longer "public" in any meaningful respect. They are simply run by the government.

The replacement of public schools by "government schools" says everything one needs to know about the disaster that American primary and secondary education has become. The fact that so many states are considering different mechanisms to increase parental choice in education reveals the extent of concern about this problem.

The classic story of reform in this area is in East Harlem—New York School District 4. Before 1974, when a choice system was initiated, this district was a model of public school dysfunction. It ranked thirty-second out of New York's thirty-two school districts in academic achievement; it suffered high truancy rates, a graduation rate of less than 50 percent, low reading and math scores.

In the reorganized district, a huge, centrally managed school was broken up into a number of smaller schools, each governed by and responding to a much smaller group of parents and students. The schools specialized, responding to the different endowments and interests of the individual students. And over time, once they were committed to choice, the many schools in the reorganized district achieved remarkable progress. The district's graduation rate rose to more than 90 percent. Truancy declined. Reading and math scores soared, and today it ranks sixteenth out of the city's school districts in achievement. In fact, today some parents in higher-income neighborhoods of Manhattan compete to send their children there.

In education, the hostility to choice is engendered by a traditional, top-down concept of civic education, which denies the importance of freedom and is plainly inappropriate in a modern, individuated nation. Our task is to encourage participation in a common venture, built on the voluntary commitment of free people.

Teachers' unions have been the most powerful political lobby combatting choice in education—so much so that they organized an enormous effort recently in California to prevent a choice initiative from even getting on the state ballot. This is so notwithstanding the fact that, especially in the inner cities, public school teachers are victims no less than are parents and students of the top-heavy, bureaucratic educational system. I believe that the teachers' opposition to choice or voucher systems may come primarily from fear generated by the way in which the advocates of choice argue their case. Many advocates, encouraged especially by economists, couch their appeals negatively, as ensuring competition among schools. Thus they emphasize how choice systems will force bad schools out of business. They would probably get a more sympathetic hearing from teachers by emphasizing the positive opportunities that choice systems would provide for people, working together, to create rewarding educational experiences. Such systems would allow teachers to participate as professionals, rather than as employees of large bureaucracies, and to work in cooperative partnership with parents, inspired by common concern for children.

Most choice initiatives openly push for individuals' right to leave the public schools. The experiences of New York School District 4 and of its sister, School District 3—more recently committed to choice—show how it may be easiest to establish choice by working within existing institutional frameworks. In the end, this is proving to be a more successful strategy than trying to introduce a universal program of "public" vouchers that would, in effect, instantly privatize all public education. Around the country, a growing number of schools are applying for the right to be operated as substantially independent of their school districts.

Virtually all of the states that are now considering choice systems plan to limit choice to the public schools. A major reason for the limitation is political: because it is easier to get public school establishment support for it. For example, both Bill Honig, former superintendent of the California state school system, and Albert Shanker, head of the American Federation of Teachers, support choice as long as it is limited to public schools.

But if citizens cannot use vouchers to go to private schools, then a situation will continue to exist in which only the rich can buy their way out of the "public" system if it is not working for them. Why should we reserve this right only for people who can afford to pay twice for their children's education—once in taxes to support government schools and again for private tuition?

In effect, the limitation of full choice to the rich implies that tax revenues are the property of a government that is somehow separate and distinct from the people who elect and support it. Such a relationship is more appropriate to feudalism than it is to a democracy. It gives the impression that the people are the servants of the government, and thus prevents the development of real community. It is the ultimate debasement of democratic government.

The real objection to including private schools in a choice system grows from a more general concern about the potentially negative side of self-governance. The implication is that if we let people control their own lives, they will do "antisocial" things. The most iniquitous of these would be active efforts to exclude people of other races, religions, and so on. The concern also includes fears that the poorest, most economically disadvantaged people would be left behind. It is easiest to guard against such abuses by allowing only accredited schools into the choice system: schools teaching hatred or practicing discrimination would not be allowed.

Although opponents of choice always advance principled arguments supporting their opposition, their consistent and passionate rejection of vouchers and choice for the poorest students and families raises serious questions about how far their concern extends beyond self-interest.[6]

Housing

In debates over housing policy, as over education, the tension is between a "government" system and a "public" system. Government housing is run (or rather, neglected) by bureaucrats, and its projects are notable as spawning beds for crime, drug dealing, and all of the terrors associated with the inner city. Under Jack Kemp, the federal Department of Housing and Urban Development (HUD) has launched its Project HOPE, which is designed to empower tenants of government housing projects to assume control of the projects, to manage them, and eventually to own them.

A popular movement is now emerging to pursue this objective, led by an odd and extraordinary combination of conservatives, libertarians, and former New Left liberals and radicals. The leading groups promoting this new movement are the Washington-based National Center for Neighborhood Enterprise, directed by Robert Woodson, and San Francisco's Center for Self-Governance (CSG), directed by Robert B. Hawkins, Jr. Woodson's group has been engaged in the struggle for tenant management and ownership since the early 1980s, finally finding an ally in Kemp. Hawkins' organization, which was founded in 1990 and with which I am associated, is working to develop local support structures, especially among local businesses, that can supply tenants with the tools and knowledge they will need to manage their housing projects. Organizing support from local communities, especially from the business community, is necessary to making the dream of tenant management and ownership a reality.

CSG's associate, the Citizens' Alliance for Community Empowerment (CACE), is implementing a series of training programs to help tenant groups to master all aspects of management. For example, CACE enlisted the local office of Deloitte and Touche, accountants, to condense HUD's five hundred pages of accounting regulations into a simple nineteen-page handbook. CACE is also working with a group of local lawyers to help tenants to negotiate memorandums of understanding with the housing authority, and with several real estate companies to train tenants to manage the projects. Future projects include a program to offer training in leadership to members of the project boards of directors.

Governmental housing bureaucracies have not responded enthusiastically to such endeavors, which they see as a threat to their power. They have responded by running their own slates of candidates against those of the tenant groups in elections for project boards of directors, where they have been soundly beaten. They have arbitrarily moved tenants out of the projects, trying to destroy any sense of community. Such actions typify the worst behavior of the order left, whose notion it is that community can be fostered only through command, control, and coercion. Dealing with bureaucratic resistance is another, crucial task for local support organizations such as CACE.

What do these tenants want to accomplish? One of the San Francisco activists, Brenda Stringer, has said: "My goal is to pay taxes. When I pay taxes, I will know that I am a full citizen." This desire to become self-sufficient, contributing members of society is common among housing tenants. It may explain why, in 1991, precincts that include two of the projects whose tenants are working with CACE were carried by San Francisco mayoral candidate Frank Jordan, a former police chief, in his successful bid to unseat liberal incumbent Art Agnos.

Legal Services

Legal services to aid the poor in civil cases are financed largely by the national Legal Services Corporation, an independent body created and funded by Congress. In 1992 it had a budget of about $350 million, the bulk of which went to several hundred legal services programs around the country that employ staff attorneys. In addition, the corporation also finances a handful of supplementary "judicare" programs, which subsidize attorneys in private practice to represent the poor.

The program's historical bias in favor of subsidizing providers rather than recipients of legal services is evident today in comparing the two programs that exist side by side in Alameda County, California, on the east side of San Francisco Bay. The main program in the county is the Legal Aid Society of Alameda County, which maintains thirteen full-time attorneys with a $1.5 million annual budget. Alongside this is the Charles Houston Law Club, a judicare program with a budget of only $150,000. Both programs subsidize providers; even the judicare program is not a voucher program that subsidizes clients. At the same time, the bias in favor of government attorneys is explicit. Apart from the tenfold difference in overall funding, the corporation also discriminates in favor of the Legal Aid Society program by paying private judicare attorneys only $35–40 per hour, while it covers the costs of staff lawyers amounting to about $55 per hour. Moreover, since judicare payments are subject to a maximum limit of $300 per case, actual subsidies to private attorneys can fall substantially below $35 per hour.

Despite its larger budget, the Legal Aid Society provides almost no service to individual clients—that is left to the judicare program. Legal Aid focuses instead on prosecuting class-action or "impact" cases, chosen with an eye to setting new precedents in law affecting the poor.

The system of focusing subsidies on legal services provided by full-time government attorneys raises many questions: Why should low-income clients be restricted in choosing their own lawyers? Why should local attorneys not be compensated at rates at least as high as the government lawyers? Fairer compensation would encourage greater participation by the local bar, especially minority-group attorneys in counties with large minority populations (nearly half the population of Alameda County is nonwhite).

Subsidizing clients would increase their say in how legal service programs are run—giving them a voice in establishing priorities. If recipients of legal services had a say, it is hard to believe that they would choose to spend as little as 10 percent of program moneys to provide service to individual clients.

A concrete benefit from expansion of judicare would be the support it would provide to the local private bar, the members of which form a substantial portion of the minority-group leadership class. Many minority attorneys who would like to serve the communities they come from find that, unless they are willing to work full time as government attorneys, they cannot sustain a practice. So they work for large corporations and in other kinds of government work. Increasing their opportunities to serve low-income individuals as private practitioners would expand choices for all.

Finally, why should only government lawyers have opportunities to prosecute "impact" cases? Encouraging the monopolization of such noteworthy cases by government lawyers, many of them from outside the communities involved, is, in a sense, imperialistic. Why should local private attorneys not be able to compete to work on the impact cases that affect their own communities?

I became aware of the potential of the judicare approach in the early 1970s, when I was working for the California State Office of Economic Opportunity. I arranged to meet with two prominent black lawyers in Oakland to discuss a proposed study of the impact of publicly funded legal services on low-income and minority communities. We met in the office of Robert Harris, then president of the National Bar Association (the principal national organization of black lawyers). Also present was Howard Moore, an attorney for communist revolutionary Angela Davis.

The purpose of the meeting was to engage these men's cooperation in a study of how the public legal services system was affecting two groups: low-income, largely black, neighborhoods, and the black legal community. I wanted to address the effects of employing government lawyers, often from outside the community, to serve low-income clients at no charge, thus discouraging those clients from seeking the counsel of privately employed black lawyers.

My suspicion was that the program not only separated the community from an important part of its potential leadership class, but also encouraged the perception that black private lawyers sought to rip off their clients by charging for services (there was no judicare program then). Beyond this, all available anecdotal evidence pointed to the conclusion that the program was making it hard for lawyers from minority groups in private practice to make a living.

I presented the judicare alternative. When I had finished, Moore broke the long silence that followed: "Let me be sure I understand this correctly," he began. "Are you telling us that a conservative, white agency [the state OEO] working for a conservative, white governor [Reagan] wants to reform the legal services program and let people from the local community control it?"

Yes, I said, that is what I was proposing. A small caveat, I said, was that under the new system local private lawyers would not "control" the program in the way that the poverty lawyers had always done. Rather, control would pass to clients—ordinary people who needed legal services—who could then decide what kind of service they desired and which attorney they wanted to use. Local lawyers could then compete for business, including opportunities to prosecute class-action impact cases, which would be funded by a specifically earmarked percentage of program funds.

The two lawyers enjoyed what seemed to them an incredible irony. The idea of whites of any political stripe wanting to give blacks real control over their own lives seemed a surprise; but for white conservatives, working for Ronald Reagan, to propose it seemed surreal.

Once they got used to the idea, however, their conversation moved in a radically different direction. They confided how difficult it was for them personally to practice law in competition against the "free" service given by government poverty lawyers. They said that many other black lawyers were also struggling. Moore even asserted, angrily, that radical poverty lawyers were destroying the black community, refusing to give service that real people needed and wanted, and pursuing their own causes without thinking about the people they were supposed to be serving.

I was never able to get the funding to do the study. But in the nearly twenty years that have passed since then, that meeting has continued to symbolize for me an aspiration held by many disadvantaged people: to gain some control over, and choice among, the institutions that affect their lives.

Giving lawyers from outside a community all power to decide what kind of legal services that a community will receive is a devastating form of social service paternalism. It has no place in a society committed to real participation of citizens in the institutions that affect their lives.

Delivery of Public Goods

A major purpose of the self-governance movement is to establish mechanisms to facilitate economic, social, and political decentralization.[7] Such institutions would allow local communities and governments the ability to control many if not most aspects of public administration.

This point is especially important with regard to construction of physical infrastructure, which is crucial to economic growth. In the United States a great deal of this infrastructure was built by single-purpose public sector enterprises in the form of "special districts" providing water, power, fire protection, airports, hospitals, roads, and so on. This form of administration, involving private citizens in organizing and administering community facilities and services, has been particularly common and successful in rural areas.

Special districts feature several attractions. They represent an effort by communities to invest in themselves, to provide for their own welfare. As citizen-managed entities, they can provide valuable training in self-governance; and since they have a finite purpose, they have the political advantage of not threatening other governmental entities.

The great enemy of such self-governance will always be the tradition of the strong centralized state as the source and overseer of development. Everywhere this tradition is crumbling because it denies self-governance to people who demand it.

Meeting Objections to Self-Governance

What has kept decentralization and self-governance from having greater effect on public policy? The most comprehensive obstacle, I believe, has been the negative cast of our politics—the emphasis on preventing or diminishing failure rather than allowing or reinforcing success.

This negative focus is most obvious in liberals' concern that only some people—advantaged people—will benefit from greater self-governance. Liberals are concerned that the poor and disadvantaged will not be able to take advantage of radical decentralization, and that they will be left further behind and even more disadvantaged than they are now.

I must note here again that focusing on who is "ahead" and who is "behind," as if we were all in some national footrace, implies preoccupation only with external rewards. As I discussed in Chapter 6, as long as we believe in our politics that external rewards are all that matter, we will program failure into all serious efforts to achieve social justice. Reducing the preoccupation of marginal people, especially intellectuals, with external rewards thus remains a crucial task for everyone concerned to solve the crisis in our politics.

The preoccupation with failure is especially evident in the debate over educational choice, even when it is proposed as being limited to the public schools. The fear is expressed that only the best students will be able to take advantage of choice—that they will be "skimmed off" and go to the best schools, leaving the rest behind. This is the major concern expressed about the Edison Project, directed by former Yale president Benno C. Schmidt, a private company that is exploring radical reforms of existing school formats.

Hoover Institution Fellow Thomas Sowell answers these objections by noting that they amount to a policy of holding back everyone who values education until the last person also comes to value it. The experience of School District 4 in East Harlem shows how a poor community can use choice to breathe life back into education. Similarly, Schmidt believes that the greatest opportunities for the Edison Project are in the inner cities, where parental dissatisfaction with schools is most intense.

If we look at social programs almost universally acknowledged to work, the crucial feature in all of them is emphasis on individual responsibility. One example from abroad is Bangladesh's Grameen Bank, which extends small loans (averaging about $60) to a population among the poorest in the world (average annual wage about $170). Like all successful programs, the Grameen Bank combines a belief in people, no matter how disadvantaged, with an active program of empowerment. The bank's founder Muhammad Yunus, in a book he edited, *Jorimon of Beltoil Village and Others: In Search of a Future,* describes the people, primarily rural women, the bank lends to. His portraits make clear that for them, the moment of empowerment comes not when they receive their loan; it comes when they make their first repayment.[8] It comes, that is to say, not when they receive help but when they know they can give something back. This finding provides a powerful echo to the statement of the public housing tenant in San Francisco who proclaimed her aspiration to pay taxes, which she thought essential to her feeling like a full citizen.

Similarly, Alcoholics Anonymous (AA) and Narcotics Anonymous (NA) attribute their success to their ability to encourage people—all kinds of people, the "disadvantaged" as well as the "advantaged"—to take responsibility for their own lives.

The negative goal of shielding the disadvantaged from all possible harm has inspired public institutions so overweening that they deny all but the rich an opportunity to work for and enjoy positive experiences as citizens in a community. This system has a devastating effect, foreclosing all hope of self-reliance to all those not rich enough to buy their way out.

The importance of the self-governance movement in education, housing, and other areas is that it is empowering the poor and minority-group members to demand their right to be treated as equals—forcing both the left and right to take them seriously and to empower them with control of their own lives.

Allowing and encouraging self-governance places great demands on advantaged people: it challenges them to "put up or shut up" in their protestations of concern about the disadvantaged. It challenges them to roll up their sleeves, get down to work in the disadvantaged communities, and help people acquire the basic tools that are necessary for their empowerment. It means teaching tenants in housing projects the basics of accounting and management to allow them to manage their projects. It means letting attorneys who rose from disadvantaged communities compete for public moneys that go to support legal services for low-income people. It means giving leadership training that encourages people to believe that they can control their own lives and destinies.

These are substantial challenges. It may be assumed that many people who occupy the centers of power—people working in government and in all of its attendant, ancillary institutions, including the media—will have little interest in this program. They will prefer to perpetuate the present system, which sustains their superior positions as grand chess masters, moving people around to the music provided by their high-minded moralizing.

Standing behind the current "principals" in policy making (I include both policy makers and the media in this category) is the tangle of special interest groups that benefit from the current centralized policy structure. This twisted mass, clinging to every nook and cranny of the policy mechanism, is the nemesis of both the right, which seeks to reduce government, and the left, which tries to use it more effectively.

Only radical change can counter the crisis in our politics. For that, people with power must stop trying to create political community on the cheap, at the behest of comfortable bureaucrats. Real change will not come easily: it will require far more effort than anyone has yet made.

Nevertheless, the day of self-governance is coming. And when it arrives, the crisis in our politics will be over. When it arrives, it will be delivered by a strange assortment of conservatives, liberals, and radicals—black and white, men and women, rich and poor. When it comes it will transcend all current understandings of our national politics.

A crucial melding of conservative and liberal qualities form the self-governing vision, which explains why its adherents are drawn from such an odd assortment of grass-roots activists. They all share one thing—a terminal disillusionment with the traditional politics of both parties.

The Challenge before Us

The problem of moving to a nonmechanistic conception of politics, grounded in the self-governance of individuals and communities, has two dimensions. One dimension is objective and tangible and has an institutional solution. The second dimension is subjective and intangible and can be affected only in limited ways by institutional change. This second dimension can only be addressed by a change of spirit or attitude intended to satisfy our subjective need to reconcile freedom and order.

The objective, institutional solution is relatively straightforward and easy to implement. It requires radically decentralizing both governmental and private institutions, expanding choice, and trusting people to reach out voluntarily to cooperate in common enterprise.

The subjective, conceptual dimension of our political problem is more difficult to confront, even to understand, in part because we have no language to talk about it. Grappling with this more profound, subjective side will require appreciation of how advancing consciousness of the self is changing all dimensions of both individual and social life—destroying tradition and creating the need for new forms of value and authority, intensifying alienation and the need for connection, increasing emphasis on external rewards and (therefore) the sense of social inequality, intensifying the need for conscious engagement in all dimensions of life, and with it demands for self-governance. Understanding the full dimensions of our subjective dilemma is far beyond the scope of this book, but our ability to solve that dilemma will ultimately determine the future of our democratic institutions and politics.

Pieces of the puzzle are already in place—at least significant interest groups have embraced their importance. Growing numbers of progressive movements—beginning with the environmentalists and now including most contemporary advocates of the disadvantaged—are focusing more and more on subjective, conceptual issues, and they can be counted on to take up the challenge.

In trying to find a new path, our greatest task is to move beyond the scientific method, on which we have modeled our politics. Understanding truth scientifically—negatively—militates against efforts to create a sense of community that integrates our needs for freedom and order. It also blinds us to the degree to which such integration must include the best of the left and the right. Without such integration, we will be doomed to a continuing nightmare of conflict, and self-governance will remain only a dream.

Postscript

For hundreds of years Western thought has seen objective knowledge as the only legitimate end of reasoned inquiry, and rational and intellectual concepts have continued to dominate the structure of our political system up to the present day. What has not yet been recognized is that the same forces that began at the end of the Middle Ages to sweep religion aside in favor of science are now calling science and objectivity into question. Advancing consciousness of the self first led men to reject the preconscious world of religion, and to focus on achieving economic, social, and political *ends* in their quest to understand and then conquer the objective world. Now the further advance of self-consciousness is leading men inward again, toward the world of subjectivity and an emphasis on the *means* of living. First came consciousness of individuality, and with it a strong impulse to explore the objective world. As individualism developed, subjective alienation—a painful sense of the separation of the individual from community—appeared. This alienation, now widespread, is producing a growing political concern and even preoccupation with ways to reconnect the individual and his community—to reconcile freedom and order.

Although the changes in the political atmosphere have been

enormous in the past three decades, governments and politicians have not responded. And thus we have come to feel an alarming despondency about our organized political life. Our leaders do not often address our need for a more subjective, participatory politics, because they have no idea how to do so.

The ephemeral confidence and optimism Americans felt after the victory in the Gulf War indicates that their abiding concern lies with much deeper issues. The second Russian "revolution" and the end of the Cold War killed the rationale for a state built around a concern for national security, and none of the presidential candidates in the 1992 election suggested a convincing alternative foundation for strong, central government authority. Skepticism about the benefits of centralization, therefore, remains high. Under the circumstances, it is no surprise that many voters told pollsters that they would have voted no to all of the candidates, had that option been open to them.

One way to think about our dilemma is to consider the extraordinary and almost complete separation that exists between the way we think about, talk about, and behave in our *public* and our *private* lives. The most striking differences lie in the way we judge value and in the language we use to describe it. The differences are evident in our efforts at both celebration and criticism—in our judgments of both good and bad.

These differences show up in our attitude toward means and ends. The achievement of ends is what matters in public discourse; the means by which we go about our lives matter to us in private. In our private lives, we celebrate the *process* of living, independent of concern for ends. Especially, we enjoy the conduct of personal relationships for their own sake. Healthy people understand that relationships with loved ones, opportunities for recreation and creative expression, and other intangibles are the most important contributors to a "happy life."

We might say that the things that matter most to us privately are those we feel and understand subjectively, rather than the realities we define objectively. As subjective beings, our impulse is to connect with others, with nature, with the world and cosmos beyond. I have referred to this impulse as the desire to "live through means," to concentrate on the process of living.

Our public life could not be more different. In politics our preoccupation is entirely with ends, defined objectively—with what causes to fund, with what bills will be passed, with what goals the president will favor. At the same time, policy and opinion makers seem oddly unaware that public alienation from centralized government is caused by the failure to provide people with subjectively satisfying means of participation and self-governance.

Marginal people—intellectuals and artists, and often the young—stand in ambivalent and often tormented relation to these issues. On the one hand, as I have argued, they are the greatest force in society promoting the emphasis on external rewards. Their focus on external rewards reveals their preoccupation with ends. Yet their dependence on external rewards is entirely unsatisfying, and this explains why marginal people are also leading our political debate away from preoccupation with the objective and with ends, and are leading it toward a rediscovery of a satisfying internal standard of values. They are doing this by recasting our definition of social disadvantage in increasingly subjective terms and promoting a view of the environment that is more concerned with changing how we relate to nature than with how we manage resources.

Science and intellect are restricted to defining truth and knowledge negatively. They comprehend truth only in terms of what is not false; they cannot affirm anything as positively true. It is not surprising that growing numbers of people are finding that this is simply not enough. They are turning inward in search of positive visions of what is true. The most powerful of those visions in politics is the need of people for control of their own lives—the need to cooperate with others for a common purpose. Only a politics that concentrates on the means of participation and self-governance can have hope of allowing people positive experiences in community, and only this can provide hope of ending the crisis in our politics.

In their changing attitudes about the disadvantaged and their concern about man's relation to nature, marginal intellectuals are increasingly moving to the politics and idealism of means in order to satisfy their subjective need for reconnection.

The intensity of the need of marginal people to reconnect became clear to me a couple of years ago when I witnessed an extraordinary incident at the inaugural conference of the U.S. Institute for Peace. One of the purposes of the conference was to bring together all types of foreign policy makers and commentators, both "hawks" and "doves." Halfway into the event, when everything was going smoothly, one of the hawks remarked that he thought the Nobel Peace Prize should go to the Stinger missile, which, he asserted, had ended the war in Afghanistan.

That single remark destroyed the conference. It did so because it mocked and utterly devastated the basic dovish position, which saw arms reductions as the key to peace. At that moment, therefore, all possibility for dialogue between the two groups died, and the doves were as shattered and angry as the hawks were exultant.

To understand what happened, one must begin by recognizing that the contention about the Stinger missile was accurate. At least it was *taken* to be accurate by both sides at the conference. Unfortunately, the peace activists took no satisfaction from this example of a simple cessation of hostilities because their purpose was not to establish a *negative* concept of peace (i.e., an armistice). It was (and is) to find a *positive* means of peacekeeping that would make weapons unnecessary. They were chiefly angry because they could not articulate this ideal. The reason they could not, as Berkeley classicist and pacifist Michael Nagler argued at the end of the conference, is that they, too, had theretofore limited their arguments to a negative definition of peace (the absence of killing, the destruction of weapons).

The doves were unable to say why the mere suspension of combat did not satisfy them because they were not clear about their own, positive mission, which is to rediscover what it is to be peaceful in a positive sense. Ironically, the remark to which they took such exception did not touch their underlying concern, because it could not. This is because a positive vision of peace requires a peace process, a means. Lacking a vocabulary to articulate the distinction between ends and means, the peace activists' response to the remark could only be anger and frustration.

Environmentalists face the same dilemma. Although their political arguments are cast negatively, as when they warn against ecological catastrophe, their real concern is for a positive search for a means of relating to, even serving, nature.

Again, however, we have no language to talk about the means they seek. So environmentalists are forced to make utilitarian appeals in the idiom of economics and science in order to express their opposition to utilitarianism, economics, and science. It is a philosophically hopeless enterprise.

I have argued that the underclass is also a problem for which solutions can only be found in the realm of means, rather than ends. This problem is unique to individualistic societies, which tend to use the attainment of external rewards (material ends) to define personal identity and worth. Those who end up at the bottom of society's competitive heap become the underclass—"failures" who are regarded as incapable of helping themselves. Since no ends-focused policy can make everyone above average in status, our only hope is to reduce the importance of the external rewards by which we measure status. Traditionally, the left has tried to do this by confiscating and redistributing rewards. Wherever this is tried, it drives people and economies underground, because the valuation of external rewards continues. Although liberals still hope to use steeply progressive tax systems to achieve their goals, tax rates have declined steeply throughout the world in response to both popular demand and economic necessity.

To find a new approach we must begin by understanding that our emphasis on external rewards is a result of our modern and individualistic focus on the attainment of ends. No solution to the problem of an underclass, therefore, can be found by artificially redistributing income or enforcing equal economic or educational achievement. It can only come if we rediscover the essential value of means—the internal standard we know in our private lives but have not extended to our public and professional ones.

These lessons are especially important for marginal intellectuals, since the preoccupation with ends is most acute for them—as evidenced by their obsession with external rewards, particularly fame. The reason intellectuals suffer this obsession is that they are more individuated than other people and are thus further removed from traditional sources of meaning.

We cannot solve any of these problems as long as we lack a language to consider the subjective value of means. As long as we cannot even *talk* about the subjective interpretation of social problems and their possible solutions, we must conclude that announcements of Marxism's demise are premature. Unless we discover a non-Marxist politics that satisfies marginal people's need for reconnection and engagement, the illusory promises of socialism will continue to beckon.

It is likely that, however turned off to politics people seem now, sometime in the future a new politics will appear. Unless we change our priorities, it will be a millenarian politics, offering collectivist solutions to be enforced by all the power of the centralized state. Such a politics will be a religion of desperation, but it will win large numbers of adherents unless we can satisfy people's longing for community otherwise. Until we can find a way to talk about means, marginal intellectuals will continue to look to mechanistic, external, and objective answers for problems that are internal and subjective—answers that must, by definition, fail.

The ultimate question goes to the problem of authority. What form of authority, if any, might appeal to people afflicted with the marginal need to question traditional values? What framework of values might win such people's consent, bearing in mind that marginal people cannot be motivated merely by the dictates of tradition?

Our stake in finding answers to these questions, which raise the most basic issues of freedom and order, is very great. For unless we can find a source of authority that responds to marginal people's increasing need to understand and choose their own values (rather than simply to accept them blindly), then we may not be able to avoid the redemption that only the barrel of a gun will seem to offer.

Notes

Chapter 1, Freedom and Order

1. Alexis de Tocqueville, *Democracy in America* [1835], ed. J. P. Mayer and Max Lerner (New York: Harper and Row, 1966), I:11.

2. Hegel is an obvious choice here—and, in this century, Eric Voegelin.

3. Quoted in Kenneth Minogue, "Conservatism," *The Encyclopedia of Philosophy* (New York: Macmillan, 1972), I and II:195.

Chapter 2, Conservatives Return to Freedom

1. William F. Buckley, Jr., *Did You Ever See a Dream Walking? American Conservative Thought in the Twentieth Century* (New York: Bobbs-Merrill, 1970), xvii.

2. Reprinted in "Reformers Control New Hungary Party," *San Francisco Chronicle,* October 10, 1989, sec. A, p. 15. Italics added.

3. Friedman said this to me in a personal conversation.

4. Irving Kristol, *Confessions of a Neoconservative* (New York: Basic Books, 1983), 39.

5. Friedrich A. Hayek, *The Constitution of Liberty* (Chicago: University of Chicago Press, 1960), 61.

6. Edmund Burke, "A Letter to a Member of the National Assembly" [1791], in *The Works of Edmund Burke,* 7th ed. (Boston: Little, Brown, 1881), IV:52.

7. A. Lawrence Chickering and Mohamed Salahdine, eds., *The Silent Revolution: The Informal Sector in Five Asian and Near Eastern Countries* (San Francisco: ICS Press, 1991).

Chapter 3, Liberals Opt for Order

1. Tom Wolfe, *The Painted Word* (New York: Farrar, Straus and Giroux, 1975).

2. See, e.g., John D. Rockefeller III, speech to the Society of the Family of Man, October 23, 1968, reprinted as "In Praise of Young Revolutionaries," *Saturday Review,* December 14, 1968. An excerpt from Mr. Rockefeller's speech will provide a sense of what I am talking about:

> Instead of worrying about how to suppress the youth revolution we of the older generation should be worrying about how to sustain it. The student activists are in many ways the elite of our young people. They perform a service in shaking us out of our complacency. . . .
>
> To achieve such action we of the older generation must re-examine our attitudes, our assumptions and our goals. We must take as seriously as do the young the great Judeo-Christian values of our heritage. We must be as dedicated as they in fighting injustices and improving our laws.

3. William O. Douglas, *Points of Rebellion* (New York: Random House, 1970), 95.

4. Jean-Paul Sartre, preface to Frantz Fanon, *The Wretched of the Earth* [1961], trans. Constance Farrington (New York: Grove Press, 1968), 17. Italics added.

5. "Asian Tragedy," *Ramparts,* March 1972, 6.

6. William Appleman Williams, "Just Who Is Nixon Anyway?" *New York Review of Books,* February 24, 1972, 7ff.

7. Quoted in Stanley Rothman and Robert Lichter, *Roots of Radicalism* (New York: Oxford University Press, 1982), 21.

8. Ibid., 19–21.

Chapter 4, Order without Collectivism

1. Quoted in John B. Judis, *William F. Buckley, Jr.* (New York: Simon and Schuster), 166.

2. Karl Marx and Friedrich Engels, *The Communist Manifesto* [1848] trans. Samuel Moore (Chicago: Regnery Gateway, 1982), 18. Italics added.

3. Mr. Reston said this in a CBS television interview conducted by Eric Severeid in Tokyo, following a six-week trip Reston took to China. See "Reston, Interviewed on TV, Gives Views on China Trip," *New York Times,* September 1, 1971, sec. 2, p. 4.

4. Joseph A. Schumpeter, *Capitalism, Socialism, and Democracy* (New York: Harper and Row, 1942), 127ff.

5. Irving Kristol, *Two Cheers for Capitalism* (New York: Basic Books, 1978).

Chapter 5, *The Crisis of the Centralized State*

1. "Congress's Ratings at an All-time Low," *The American Enterprise,* December 1992, 86–87.

2. For example, a CBS News/*New York Times* survey released on October 24, 1992, reported that only 22 percent of those polled said that the federal government can be trusted "to do what is right" always or most of the time, compared with 76 percent who said it will do what is right some of the time or never.

3. Irving Kristol, "About Equality," *Commentary,* November 1972, 41.

4. Lester Thurow, "Toward a Definition of Economic Justice," *The Public Interest* (Spring 1973), 79.

5. Vincent Ostrom, "Cryptoimperialism, Predatory States, and Self-Governance," in V. Ostrom, David Feeny, and Hartmut Picht, eds. *Rethinking Institutional Analysis and Development* (San Francisco: ICS Press, 1988), 43–68.

6. See Francis Fukuyama, "The End of History?" *The National Interest,* no. 16 (Summer 1989).

Chapter 6, *The Social Agenda*

1. See, e.g., James Q. Wilson, *Essays on Character* (Washington, D.C.: American Enterprise Institute, 1991).

2. For a general discussion of these issues, see George de Vos and Marcello Suarez-Orozco, *Status Inequality: The Self in Culture* (Newbury Park, Calif.: Sage Publications, 1990).

3. See Thomas Sowell, *The Economics and Politics of Race: An International Perspective* (New York: William Morrow and Co., 1983), 200.

4. John Kenneth Galbraith, "The New Position of Poverty," in Burton Weisbrod, ed., *The Economics of Poverty: An American Paradox* (Englewood Cliffs, N.J.: Prentice-Hall, 1965), 50.

5. Norman Podhoretz, *Making It* (New York: Harper and Row, 1967), xiv. Italics added.

6. See, e.g., Edward Banfield, *The Unheavenly City* [1968], 2nd ed. (Boston: Little, Brown, 1970), and Daniel P. Moynihan, ed., *Understanding Poverty* (New York: Basic Books, 1969).

7. Excellent statements of the two arguments may be found in Banfield, *The Unheavenly City,* and in a paper by Lee Rainwater in Moynihan, *Understanding Poverty.*

8. On the effect of tax rates on poverty, see Michael J. Boskin and Charles McLure, Jr., *World Tax Reform: Case Studies of Developed and Developing Countries* (San Francisco: ICS Press, 1990); on the effect of regulations, see Charles Schultze, *The Public Use of Private Interest* (Washington, D.C.: The Brookings Institution, 1977).

9. See Robert Nozick, *Anarchy, State, and Utopia* (New York: Basic Books, 1974), 242–46.

10. See Tom Wolfe, *Radical Chic and Mau-Mauing the Flak Catchers* (New York: Farrar, Straus and Giroux, 1970).

11. Wolfe, *The Painted Word,* 22–23.

12. See Jacob Burckhardt, *The Civilization of the Renaissance in Italy* [1860], trans. S. G. C. Middlemore (New York: Harper and Row, 1958), 151.

Chapter 7, The Dilemma of the "Authentic Black"

1. K. R. Minogue, *The Liberal Mind* (London: Methuen, 1963), 8–13.

2. See Stephen L. Carter, *Reflections of an Affirmative Action Baby* (New York: Basic Books, 1991); Richard Rodriguez, *Hunger of Memory* (New York: David R. Godine, 1982); and Shelby Steele, *The Content of Our Character* (New York: St. Martin's Press, 1990).

3. Kenneth Clark and Carl Gershman, "The Black Plight: Class or Race?" *New York Times Magazine,* October 5, 1980, 22–26.

4. Derrick Bell, *Faces at the Bottom of the Well: The Permanence of Racism* (New York: Basic Books, 1992).

5. Sowell, *The Economics and Politics of Race,* 200–201.

6. Rodriguez, *Hunger of Memory,* 162–72.

7. See Timothy Egan, "Defiantly Incorrect," *New York Times Magazine,* June 7, 1992, 20–21.

Chapter 8, Environmental Schizophrenia

1. Al Gore, *Earth in the Balance* (New York: Penguin, 1992).

2. For a general discussion of these issues, see John Baden and Richard L. Stroup, *Bureaucracy Versus the Environment: The Environmental Costs of Bureaucratic Governance* (Ann Arbor: University of Michigan Press, 1981).

3. On the causes of world deforestation, see, e.g., Malcolm Gillis and Robert Repetto, *Deforestation and Economic Policy,* International Center for Economic Growth Occasional Paper no. 8 (San Francisco: ICS Press, 1988).

4. See Robert A. Nisbet, *The Quest for Community* [1953] (San Francisco: ICS Press, 1990).

5. George Orwell, *The Road to Wigan Pier* [1937] (New York: Harcourt Brace Jovanovich, 1958), 189–90.

6. Quoted in Edith Efron, *The Apocalyptics: How Environmental Politics Controls What We Know about Cancer* (New York: Simon and Schuster, 1985), 28–29.

7. Ibid., 29.

8. See Stanley Rothman and Robert Lichter, "Elite Ideology and Risk Perception in Nuclear Energy Policy," *American Political Science Review* 81, no. 2 (June 1987): 383–404.

9. Ibid.

10. See Bernard L. Cohen, *The Nuclear Energy Option* (New York: Plenum Press, 1990). Interestingly, the principal publication of the antinuclear Union of

Concerned Scientists, *The Risks of Nuclear Power Reactors: A Review of the NRC Safety Study WASH–1400 (NUREG–75/014)* (Cambridge, Mass.: 1977), gave estimates only 100 times as great as these. On this basis, extrapolating from its estimates, the Union of Concerned Scientists would calculate risks equivalent to an increase in the speed limit to 55.4 miles per hour.

11. Quoted in David Bodansky, "Risk Assessment and Nuclear Power," *The Journal of Contemporary Studies* (Winter 1982), 13.

12. For a general cultural analysis of the issue, see Mary Douglas and Aaron Wildavsky, *Risk and Culture* (Berkeley: University of California Press, 1983).

13. Bruce N. Ames, "Dietary Carcinogens and Anti-carcinogens," *Science*, September 23, 1983, 1249, 1256–64. See also "Letters," *Science*, May 18, 1984.

14. I want to hold these things, which I now think indispensable. A. Lawrence Chickering, "Why Are There No Poor People in the Sierra Club?" in *No Land Is an Island* (San Francisco: Institute for Contemporary Studies, 1975), 87–91.

Chapter 9 is not annotated.

Chapter 10, Rethinking Basic Issues

1. Lionel Trilling, *Sincerity and Authenticity* [1972] (New York: Harcourt Brace Jovanovich, 1980).

2. See Stanley Milgram, *Obedience to Authority* (New York: Harper Torchlight, 1983).

Chapter 11, Political Crisis and the Centralized State

1. Quoted in William Ker Muir, Jr., *The Bully Pulpit: The Presidential Leadership of Ronald Reagan* (San Francisco: ICS Press, 1992), 89–90.

2. Seymour Martin Lipset and William Schneider, *The Confidence Gap* [1983], rev. ed. (Baltimore: The Johns Hopkins University Press, 1987).

3. For a fuller discussion, see Peter L. Berger, *The Heretical Imperative* (Garden City, N.Y.: Anchor Press/Doubleday, 1979).

4. See Nathan Glazer, *Affirmative Discrimination: Ethnic Inequality and Public Policy* (New York: Basic Books, 1975) or, more recent, John H. Bunzel, "Affirmative Action Admissions: How It Works at U.C. Berkeley," *The Public Interest*, no. 93 (Fall 1988), 111–129.

5. See Denis T. Doyle and David P. Kearns, *Winning the Brain Race: A Bold Plan to Make Our Schools Competitive* (San Francisco: ICS Press, 1991), 44.

6. See, e.g., Reynolds Holding, "Poor Parents Sue for School Vouchers," *San Francisco Chronicle*, January 4, 1993, sec. A, p. 1.

7. See, e.g., Vincent Ostrom, *The Meaning of American Federalism: Constituting a Self-Governing Society* ((San Francisco: ICS Press, 1991).

8. Muhammad Yunus, *Jorimon of Beltoil Village and Others: In Search of a Future* [1982] trans. Syed Manzoorul Islam and Arifa Rahman (Dhaka, Bangladesh: Grameen Bank, 1984), 47–52.

Index

of affirmative action, 118
national drug policy as example of,
112–13
Cold War, end of, 2–3, 200
Collectivism
new conservative idealism and, 35
order left's and order right's
preference for, 59–60
socialists' disillusionment with,
64
Communications, substitution of
custom with, 179–80
Communism, core and marginal
forms of, 150–51
The Communist Manifesto (Karl Marx
and Friedrich Engels), 62
The Confidence Gap (Seymour Martin
Lipset and William Schneider),
177
Congress, U.S., 75, 77
Conservatism
collectivist trend within, 59–60
conflicting meanings of term, 6–7,
21–22
culture of poverty and, 98
equality for minority groups and,
96
evolution of concept of, 16
fear of subjectivity by, 167
freedom vs. order within, 17,
25–26, 60
marginal within, 153–54
in Marxist countries, 24, 40
mundane view of
environmentalism and, 124
new idealism of, 34–37
order capitalism and, 66
role of freedom in, 22–27
traditional approach to social
problems by, 89–90
view of idealized past by, 159
See also Libertarianism;
Neoconservatism
The Constitution of Liberty (Edmund
Burke), 31–32
Consumer goods, marginality and,
148
The Content of Our Character (Shelby
Steele), 114
Cooperation, 10
Core
authoritarianism and, 168, 169

contemporary search for freedom
by, 170
definition, 140
for marginal conservatives, 153–54
marginal people's opposition to
and dependence on, 142–44
people associated with, 141
politics and, 150–53
relativity of, 143
symbols of, 146–48
Cornell University, 142
Corporations, failure to use
communications and decline of
large, 180
Corruption, government, 84
Counterculture, 16, 17, 39, 41, 64, 66,
100
CSG. *See* Center for Self-Governance
Cultural values, 1960s and changes in,
44
Cuomo, Mario, 175–76

Dante, 103
Davis, Angela, 47, 191
Decentralization, self-governance and,
87
Decter, Midge, 28
Delancey Street Foundation, 36
Democracy in America (Alexis de
Tocqueville), 11
Democratic convention (1968), 5–6
Democratic convention (1992), 81
Democratic party, 3, 39, 64, 81–82,
181
Deng Xiaoping, 152
Department of Housing and Urban
Development (HUD), 188, 189
Descartes, René, 144
de Soto, Hernando, 35–36, 55, 183
Deukmejian, George, 147
Did You Ever See a Dream Walking?
(William F. Buckley, Jr.), 21
Disadvantaged
affirmative action and concept of,
115–18
changing definition of, 108–10
intellectuals' commitment to, 152
liberals' concern with, 94
need to develop subjective concept
of, 137
Dostoyevsky, Fyodor, 15, 31
Douglas, William O., 48

Poverty, 90
  absolute vs. relative, 92–94
  conception of disadvantage and,
    108–10
  debate over culture of, 98
  failure of government actions to
    alleviate, 101–2
Preindividualistic state, 162–63
Private institutions, loss of confidence
  in major, 177
Private schools, choice and, 187–88
Profit, 69–70
Programs, left's belief in, 179–80
Project HOPE, 188
Protestantism, 149
Psychology, 173
Public services, providing vs.
  delivering of, 183–84

The Quest for Community (Robert
  Nisbet), 129

Race riots, 49
Racism, 113, 114
Radon, 134–35
Ramparts, 50–51
Rand, Ayn, 33, 72
Reagan, Ronald, 5, 22–23, 26, 56, 81,
  141, 159, 182, 192
Realism, conservatism and, 34
Regulation, federal, 182
Reich, Charles, 46
Reid, Ogden, 52
Relationships, personal, 178–79
Religion, 32
  core and marginal within, 146–47,
    149
  philosophy's similarity to, 12
  political debate's similarity to
    moralizing by traditional, 171
  reforms and attempts to broaden
    appeal of, 169–70
  socialism as substitute for, 60
Renaissance, 162
Republican convention (1992), 23, 26,
  81
Republican party, 17, 82, 181
Responsibility. *See* Personal
  obligation/responsibility
Reston, James, 62
Revolutionary despotism, 168, 169

Rewards, external. *See* External
  rewards
Right. *See* Conservatism
Rockefeller, John D., III, 206n2
Rodriguez, Richard, 115–18
Roman Catholic Church, 45, 149
Romantic movement, 41, 166, 172–73
Rossiter, Clinton, 22
Rousseau, Jean-Jacques, 59, 158–59,
  169
Russia, 143. *See also* Soviet Union

Salahdine, Mohamed, 36, 183
San Francisco Zen Center, 145
Sartre, Jean-Paul, 48
Savio, Mario, 53
Schneider, William, 177
School choice, 185–88
Schumacher, E. F., 70
Schumpeter, Joseph, 63, 72
Science, 199, 201
Scientific method, 162, 166
Self-consciousness. *See*
  Subjectivity/self-consciousness
Self-governance, 9–10, 85–86
  among minority groups, 119, 181
  centralized state's discouragement
    of, 175–77
  in delivery of public goods, 193
  in education, 185–88
  in entrepreneurial companies, 180
  in housing, 188–90
  integration of freedom and order
    and, 15–18, 82
  in legal services, 190–93
  libertarianism's alliance with left in
    attempts at creating, 55
  local social programs as examples
    of, 76
  in low-income and minority-group
    communities, 181
  meeting objections to, 193–96
  new conservative idealism and, 35
  problems associated with moving
    to, 87
  public services and, 183–86
  self-consciousness and, 85, 136
  subjectivity and, 172–73
Self-transcendence, longing for,
  30–31
Shanker, Albert, 187
Silbert, Mimi, 183

About the Author

A. Lawrence Chickering is founder and associate director of the International Center for Economic Growth (ICEG). After graduating from Phillips Academy (Andover), Stanford University, and Yale Law School, he worked as an associate of *National Review* and assistant to its editor, William F. Buckley, Jr. In 1974 he helped found the Institute for Contemporary Studies, a public policy think tank in California, and served as its executive editor, overseeing its publication of public policy studies. He has edited or co-edited four books, including a collection of papers on public policy issues in the 1980s. Mr. Chickering has written widely on public policy issues, especially in relation to society's underlying values. He served as a member of the National Council on the Humanities from 1981 to 1987 and served as its vice chairman from 1985 to 1987. Mr. Chickering lives in San Francisco with his wife and three of their children.